VANISHING TREASURES OF THE PHILIPPINE RAIN FOREST

Vanishing
Treasures of

Lawrence R. Heaney and Jacinto C. Regalado, Jr.

the Philippine

Rain Forest

The Field Museum, Chicago

ACKNOWLEDGMENTS AND CREDITS

This book is published by The Field Museum, Chicago, on the occasion of "Vanishing Treasures of the Philippine Rain Forest" and "Voyage of a Nation: The Philippines" —two exhibitions celebrating the biological diversity and culture of the Philippines.

PROJECT MANAGER:
Sophia Shaw
EDITOR:
Ron Dorfman
PRODUCTION MANAGER:
Sarah E. Guernsey
DESIGN AND TYPESETTING:
Joan Sommers Design
COLOR SEPARATIONS:
Professional Graphics
PRINTING AND BINDING:
Arnaldo Mondadori Editore, S.p.A.

ISBN 0-914868-19-5

♻ Printed on recycled paper.

The Field Museum
Roosevelt Road
    at Lake Shore Drive
Chicago, Illinois 60605-2496

COVER: The Philippine eagle, one of the most spectacular and endangered inhabitants of the rain forest.

ALTHOUGH THIS BOOK was written by two people, it is the product of many years of work by many individuals; to all, we wish to express our heartfelt thanks. For assistance with field investigations, often under challenging conditions, we thank all of the hundreds of people who have kindly helped us to reach our study sites and live in the forest. We have been fortunate to be part of a group of wonderful collaborators on the research that lies behind this book; Nonito Antoque, Danny Balete, Boying Fernandez, Pedro Gonzales, Paul Heideman, Nina Ingle, Steve Goodman, Eric Rickart, Blas Tabaranza, and Ruth Utzurrum made especially great contributions to field work, and to many aspects of subsequent studies as well. Angel C. Alcala and the staff and students at Silliman University provided crucial assistance to Heaney in the early stages of his studies. Members of the Wildlife Conservation Society of the Philippines all deserve thanks for their enthusiastic support of our work. The Protected Areas and Wildlife Bureau of the Philippine Department of Environment and Natural Resources and the Philippine National Museum have provided permits, information, and support for our studies; we especially thank Wilfrido Pollisco, Corazon Catibog-Sinha, Samuel Penafiel, Alma Ballesfin, Jean Caleda, Carlo Custodio, Josie DeLeon, and Marlynn Mendoza at the DENR, and Pete Gonzales at the PNM. Danny Balete, Rafe Brown, Paul Heideman, Christie Henry, Eric Rickart, and Benito Tan reviewed the manuscript; their comments and suggestions greatly enhanced the quality of the final product. We thank Rafe Brown, Keith Erickson, Tom Gnoske, Paul Heideman, William Oliver, Neil Rettig, Eric Rickart, Doel Soejarto, Benito Tan, Art Vogel, and Dave Willard for heroic efforts to provide photographs on a tight schedule; and Clara Simpson for the wonderful maps, charts, and graphs. Howie Severino, Danny Balete, and Jodi Sedlock helped with text and illustrations. Production of the book would not have been possible without the remarkable efforts of Ron Dorfman, Sarah Guernsey, Sophia Shaw, and Joan Sommers. To all of those named, and the many others whom we have not listed individually but who have given us assistance and friendship, we express our deepest gratitude.

The Ellen Thorne Smith and Marshall Field Funds of The Field Museum, the National Science Foundation, the National Cancer Institute, and the John D. and Catherine T. MacArthur Foundation provided funding for most aspects of the field studies.

Dori Soler first urged us to write this book, and we thank her for her persistence. Christie Henry provided important encouragement. We would also like to acknowledge the Field Museum officials who paved the way for the project, including Peter Crane, Laura Gates, Melissa Hilton, and Willard E. White.

PICTURE CREDITS

The Field Museum thanks the following individuals and agencies for permission to reproduce copyrighted materials in this book. Page numbers are listed below; when a number appears without a letter, the individual receives credit for all the images on that page. Placement of the image on a page is abbreviated by: T=top; B=bottom; L=left; R=right; C=center.

Frank Almeda: 51R; Rafe Brown: i, iiB, vBL, vii, 8B, 28, 42, 66, 72T, 77; Marian Dagosto: 9T; Keith Erickson: 17R, 18TL, 58; F.R.E.E., Ltd.: cover, 23, 39, 75; Tom Gnoske and David Willard: 8TR, 8TL, 19B, 31L, 41; Lawrence R. Heaney: 1, 2, 3, 4, 6B, 7TL, 7C, 7R, 10, 13T, 16L, 19T, 21T, 44B, 46L, 48, 60BR, 62, 67, 69B, 78, 79, 81R; Paul Heideman: iiB, 16, 17L, 18BR, 19TR, 20TL and BR, 25, 29, 33BL, 33TR, 34, 36, 43 all but BL, 44T, 45T 45BL, 47, 50, 52, 53, 54, 60BL, 64, 68, 69T, 70, 72T, 80, 81L, 82, 83, 84; J. S. H. Klompen: 24TL; Liaison International: 71; Peggy McNamara (illustrations): 10; Martin R. Motes: 43BL; William L. R. Oliver (illustrations): 13B (photo), 24, 26, 27, 29, 45TL, 45B, 56, 57, 59; Jacinto C. Regalado, Jr.: 21T, 32, 46BR; Eric A. Rickart: iiiL, 5, 7BL, 31R; Sonny Sales, 6T; Larry Secrist, © Richard Z. Chesnoff from *Philippines* (Harry Abrams, NY, 1978): iiT, 11; Jodi Sedlock (illustrations): 4; Clara Simpson (charts, maps, graphs): 14, 15, 16, 63, 65, 73, 74; Doel Soejarto: 21B, 22, 45R, 55; Blas R. Tabaranza, Jr.: 20TR; Benito C. Tan: iiiTR, 33TL, 37R, 38, 40, 46TR, 61, 72B; Art Vogel: 18C, 30, 35, 37L; John Weinstein: 60TL.

CONTENTS

PREFACE

JUNE 12 MARKS A DATE of historic significance for the people of the Philippines and for the Filipino-American community. On that day in 1898, General Emilio Aguinaldo and leading Filipino statesmen signed the Philippine Declaration of Independence from Spain, the first such declaration by an Asian colonial country. That day also ushered in a century of interaction between the Philippines and the United States.

In 1998, The Field Museum commemorates the Philippine Centennial with two special exhibitions on the culture and biological diversity of the Philippines and numerous related public programs and environmental initiatives. This celebration is an important example of The Field Museum's commitment to cultural understanding and is organized in conjunction with local, nationwide, and international Philippine Centennial events.

The Field Museum has conducted biological research on the Philippine fauna since 1896. Immediately after World War II, the Museum collaborated in a program with the Philippine National Museum and the Medical Corps of the United States Navy to rebuild the nation's biological research collections, which had been destroyed during bombing raids. Since the mid-1980s, Field Museum scientists have been involved in numerous partnerships in the Philippines. These include botanical inventories on Palawan (in collaboration with the Philippine National Herbarium and the United States National Cancer Institute); bird surveys on Sibuyan, Mount Isarog, and Mount Kitanglad; extensive research on mammalian diversity throughout the country (in collaboration with about a dozen Philippine institutions); and a training program in the conservation of biodiversity that helps Filipino scientists and agencies improve their research capabilities and design and obtain funding for conservation-related activities.

The publication of *Vanishing Treasures of the Philippine Rain Forest* continues The Field Museum's connection to the Philippines. We hope this volume generates interest in the country's amazing flora and fauna, raises awareness of the current ecological crisis, and makes evident the importance of conservation efforts to the nation's future economic and social health.

John W. McCarter, Jr.
President and CEO
The Field Museum

FOREWORD

IT WAS A GREAT EXPERIENCE for me to conduct field work from the 1950s through the 1970s in tropical rain forest in its pristine state on the Philippine islands of Bohol, Mindanao, Mindoro, Negros, and Palawan. At that time, the old-growth lowland rain forest still existed at sea level; large trees with huge buttresses and straight boles towered to 30 meters or more to form the tallest story. The crowns of the lower tree strata formed a continuous forest canopy, effectively preventing light rays from penetrating to the forest floor except in areas where the canopy was broken by fallen trees. Climbing bamboos, rattan, tree ferns, palms, and lianas were abundant and many ferns, aerial mosses, and orchids grew on tree trunks. The forest floor was often covered with decaying vegetation and leaf litter, harboring a rich assemblage of small animals and lower plants.

Beginning at about 1,000 meters, in montane forest, we saw trees that were shorter and heavily encrusted with mosses. This forest abounded in aerial ferns and screw pines, the latter growing so thick that they impeded human movement. The rain forest was always wet because of year-round rainfall, storing enormous volumes of water, and humidity was always high, from 70 to 100 percent, even during dry periods. The complex rain-forest structure provided for a large number and variety of animal micro-habitats. The relative quiet in the forest during the day was frequently broken by animal calls and sounds of animal movements and the occasional breaking of twigs and branches. It was a different story at night, when we heard a symphony of sounds made by birds, frogs, and insects.

In the Philippines, biodiversity and natural history are tightly linked with geological history. Once difficult to explain, the presence of a host of unique and unusual plant and animal species is rendered somewhat easier to understand today by the advances in our knowledge of land connections, movements and break-up of continents, formation of oceanic islands through tectonic events, and evolutionary processes leading to specialized niches of organisms in the tropics where temperatures show almost no variation throughout the year. There is great diversity in the geological histories of the many islands. Luzon and Mindanao, for example, have large areas that are more than 25 million years old, while the others are generally of more recent age, from 10 million to no more than 100,000 years. Most islands are oceanic in origin, but Palawan, Mindoro, and Panay have an Asiatic continental component. More recently, the development of glaciers in polar regions about 20,000 years ago and 160,000 years ago, which lowered the sea level by 120 meters or more, would have created five major islands—namely Greater Sulu, Greater Palawan, Greater Negros-Panay, Greater Mindanao, and Greater Luzon—and joined Palawan with Borneo, but it would not have closed the gaps between Borneo and Greater Sulu and Greater Mindanao, or between Greater Mindanao and Greater Luzon. In geologic and biogeographic terms, Palawan is not part of the Philippines but of the Greater Sunda Islands (Borneo, Java, and Sumatra), which were at times dry-land extensions of the Indochina-Malay region.

This diverse geological history provides an ideal opportunity to study evolution in action. Aside from evolutionary mechanisms promoting speciation in the rain forests, the partitioning of the Philippines into islands separated by sea barriers has contributed to the formation of endemic species (those that are unique to some specific area) through geographic isolation, thus preventing interbreeding. On large islands, populations have been isolated on mountain peaks separated by swaths of lowlands that also prevented gene flow. Resolving the details of many issues concerning biodiversity in the Philippines remains a great challenge, and will require further field and laboratory studies. Much remains to be learned.

The number of plant and animal species in the

Philippine rain forest is incompletely known. There are an estimated 13,500 plant species in Philippine forests, of which about 8,000 are flowering plants; about 3,200 are endemic. Philippine land vertebrate species number about a thousand: approximately 80 amphibians, some 240 reptiles, 556 birds (resident and migratory), and 174 mammals. These numbers will certainly be revised upwards as new species are still being discovered. In fact, we have described eight new species of forest frogs in a space of five years and Dr. Lawrence Heaney and his colleagues have reported 16 new mammal species during the last ten years. It is this exceptionally high level of endemism that is now attracting international attention. Seventy-five percent of amphibians, 70 percent of reptiles, 44 percent of birds, and 64 percent of mammals are found nowhere else in the world. Dr. Heaney believes that Philippine mammals may have the highest percentage of species endemism in the world on a hectare-for-hectare basis, and this could be true for other groups as well.

The tropical rain forest has supplied indigenous Philippine peoples with a treasure trove, including lumber, food, drinks, spices, and medicine. It is to the credit of these indigenous human communities that they traditionally used forest resources in a sustainable way. But it is a sad fact that today only remnants of this forest can be found, mostly in less accessible parts of the Philippines, especially in mountainous areas. In 1934, the total forested area was estimated at 17 million hectares, or 57 percent of the country's total land area of 30 million hectares. But in 1993, the area was reduced to 5.7 million hectares, or 19 percent of the land area, and most was secondary forest. The primary or original tropical lowland forest was only 872,000 hectares, the logged-over lowland forest about three million hectares, and the montane forest about a million hectares. Thus, only about 1.87 million hectares, about six percent, have remained as prime habitats of wildlife. The immediate reasons for the drastic reduction of the primary forest area are large-scale logging and conversion to agriculture, and are strongly associated with the rapid increase in human population, reaching about 70 million in 1997. Over 15 million upland people today threaten the survival of the remaining forests, despite government efforts at protection.

A large number of endemic species in the Philippine tropical rain forest and the forest itself are now threatened with complete destruction, making the country a "hot spot," that is, an area where there is a high probability of species extinctions. Already some 52 native vertebrate species are in the critical or endangered categories, and a great many more are listed as threatened. The frog *Platymantis spelaeus* and the fruit bat *Dobsonia chapmani* are almost surely extinct, and another frog, a bushy-tailed cloud rat, and at least one species of bird are probably extinct as well. Most endemic land vertebrates (including birds, small arboreal frogs, and many mammals) require primary-forest habitats and fail to survive in highly disturbed and secondary forests. Preservation of the primary rain forest is therefore a high priority for the Filipino people.

This book, published in connection with The Field Museum exhibits to commemorate the Philippine Centennial in 1998, is indeed a significant contribution. The authors have described the vanishing treasures of our Philippine tropical rain forest in both words and images. Both authors, scientists with long research experience in the Philippines, are eminently competent to present the case for these treasures to the readers. Drs. Heaney and Regalado deserve our commendation for writing this book with a broad audience in mind and for reminding us how much humankind will lose if the Philippine tropical rain forest is not preserved. It is my hope that through this book, readers will better understand and appreciate the role of the Philippine tropical rain forest, its biodiversity, and their impact in human affairs and that, as a result, they will contribute resources to the preservation of this forest, which still holds many secrets for us and future generations to unravel.

Angel C. Alcala, Ph.D.
Chairman
Commission on Higher Education
Republic of the Philippines

The small trees with twisted, gnarled trunks and branches are so densely covered with moss that what we thought were tree trunks often proved to be stems no thicker than a thumb surrounded by several inches of moss.

Discovering Diversity

LAWRENCE R. HEANEY

ARRIVAL ON MOUNT ISAROG

Its whiskers quivering and sweeping back and forth, the little animal in the cage was one of the oddest creatures I had ever seen. With long, narrow hind feet, hefty haunches, and small but stout forelimbs and claws, it looked a bit like a tiny kangaroo. But the small size, silvery fur, and long, delicately tapering snout tipped with tiny teeth marked it as something utterly unlike a kangaroo, or anything else. Danny, one of the young subsistence farmers we had hired to help us with trapping and camp work, had just brought it into our cluster of tarps and tents, the broad grin on his face instantly showing that he thought he had a prize for us. He was unquestionably right.

The forest on Mount Isarog in southern Luzon where we captured the animal in May 1988 is one of the most remarkable places on earth. Orchids grow everywhere, and earthworms are so abundant that their cast-off piles of dirt nearly cover the ground. The small trees with twisted, gnarled trunks and branches are so densely covered with moss that what we thought were tree trunks often proved to be stems no thicker than a thumb surrounded by several inches of moss. Even the ground is blanketed by this moss, at the top of a layer of humus two to five meters thick. Fog blows through the trees during most of the day and night, leaving everything dripping with water, and torrential rains fall frequently during most months; the total yearly rainfall can reach 12 meters, more than 12 times as much as in Seattle. Temperatures are low, never freezing but rarely warm. The diversity of plants in the habitat is stunning: On one afternoon, I counted two species of orchids, at least three kinds of ferns, two species of clubmosses, five species of mosses, and five species of saplings growing on a single log only a third of a meter long.

In April 1961, a team of field workers from Silliman University, led by Professor Dioscoro S. Rabor, had conducted the first zoological studies of Mount Isarog National Park, as part of a long-term study of birds in collaboration with several museums in the United States. In what little

Cool temperatures and high rainfall encourage the growth of moss, ferns, and orchids virtually everywhere in the mossy rain forest.

Mount Isarog, an extinct volcano that is the site of one of the oldest national parks in the Philippines. Mossy forest at the summit (RIGHT) receives up to 12 meters of rainfall per year, which is quickly absorbed by thick layers of soil rich in humus.

time could be freed from the bird studies, they set traps for small mammals, since the local species had never been surveyed previously. Professor Rabor, better known as Joe, had promised to send some rodents back to The Field Museum in Chicago, to a friend and colleague who had a special interest in Philippine rodents. The team caught more than one hundred species of birds, but had time for only a little trapping; about two dozen small rats and mice were quickly skinned and stuffed for the Museum before anyone had time to examine them closely. No notes were made describing the habitat or the odd appearance of several of the animals.

The rodent specimens were cleaned and cataloged in Chicago but sat in a cabinet unstudied, for Joe Rabor's friend, "Sandy" Sanborn, was in declining health, and died

not long after. It was not until 20 years later that two other biologists saw the specimens and realized that among them were two species of mammals completely unknown to science, each represented by a single specimen—a tiny shrew-like species and a rodent with big haunches and an exceptionally elongated snout. The biologists named the larger of the two *Rhynchomys isarogensis*, which translates as "the snout-mouse from Isarog."

The animal that Danny brought into camp that day in 1988 was the first live individual of *Rhynchomys isarogensis* ever seen by biologists. As our group of Americans and Filipinos crowded around, we felt the elation that makes the hard work of scientific field studies worthwhile. First whooping and hollering, then shushing each other to keep from startling the little critter, we all peered through the

The Isarog shrew-rat is one of the few mammals in the world to feed almost exclusively on earthworms.

wire mesh of the cage-trap with something that felt a great deal like reverence. We had rediscovered a "lost" species.

Over the next two days, we did as we typically do with live animals we have never seen before: We gave it water and some nesting material, and samples of everything we thought a rodent might eat from the surrounding forest. The little animal sniffed hopefully at small seeds, acorns, several small reddish fruits, and some tender young leaves, but clearly they were not what he was hoping for. Raw and cooked rice, bread, dried mangoes, dried fish, oatmeal, and peanut butter drew the same response. He would hop over to the side of the cage each time we held something out for him, then, almost visibly disappointed, would hop back to his nest. Hard-shelled beetles, ants, and a lightning bug drew no interest. He took a grub from the end of a pair of tweezers and ate it without any sign of enthusiasm. After 24 hours, we began to worry that he must be getting hungry.

At that point, Leoning, a subsistence farmer from Negros who had worked with us for several years, kicked over a rock next to the table, uncovering a couple of squirming earthworms. Almost as a joke, he picked one up and held it out for the little animal, who rushed to the side of the cage, pounced on the worm, held one end in his teeth while he shucked off the dirt with his paws, and then swallowed it like a long piece of spaghetti.

Shouting and laughing with excitement, we spread out to find more worms. In short order the animal devoured a half-dozen more, tearing the larger ones into pieces before swallowing them. *Rhynchomys isarogensis* had proven itself to be a primary vermivore—one of the few species of mammals to live on almost nothing but earthworms.

The Isarog shrew-rats, as we now call them, make tiny trails in the forest a few inches wide, carefully cleaned of debris. They patrol the trails day and night, and when they find an earthworm, they pounce quickly, using the long, narrow snout to poke down into the moss to get a good hold, then lift the worm high as they quickly dig it out.

This species has evolved in a direction that few biologists might have expected, but one that makes a great deal of sense: Its unusual prey is one of the most abundant resources in their habitat. That habitat is unusual in several additional ways. It has exceptionally high numbers of unique species of animals and plants, and remarkably high rainfall that promotes the development of dwarf trees, heavy moss cover, and a thick layer of soil rich in decomposing leaves, branches, and moss.

When a typhoon hits Mount Isarog directly, up to a meter of rain can fall in a day, but the high mountain forests function as a gigantic sponge, soaking up the heavy rains and releasing the water slowly into the groundwater system. This natural water-control system prevents floods, but it also prevents droughts by gradually releasing water throughout the year into springs, streams, and rivers, even during the two- to four-month dry season that occurs in the lowlands each year. The Isarog shrew-rat, the earthworms it eats, and the habitat in which they live all form part of the network of mountain rain forests that supplies one of the most critical needs of the human societies that also live in the area—clean, steadily flowing water.

On breezy days during our field studies on Mount Isarog in 1988, we could hear only the sounds of neighboring birds and frogs, as the sighing of the wind in the trees covered other sounds from farther away. On days when the wind was still we were serenaded from dawn to dusk by a different sound—the roar of chain saws and the crashing of trees echoing from lower on the slopes. We heard a dozen or more big trees being felled and cut each day, rumbling like thunder in the distance. When we visited the sites where the cut trees lay, we found young subsistence farmers, who had rented a chain saw from a local businessman with the promise to deliver timber to the nearest road, where a truck would pick up the wood. The truck would climb the mountain into the national park every few weeks, pick up lumber from enough locations to make a full load,

Clean water flows abundantly from Mount Isarog, providing much of the water for the heavily populated lowlands. But illegal logging and burning have gradually destroyed the rain forest on the lower slopes, disrupting the watershed.

then haul it to Naga City under the cover of darkness. We were told that at the check-points set up by government agencies and police, payments were made to assure that everyone received a share from the illegal logging, and the next day beautiful hardwood lumber was available at the hardware store owned by a relative of a prominent local politician. After paying for the loan of the chain saws, the subsistence farmers who did the difficult and dangerous work of cutting the trees received the equivalent of a few dollars per day, and those receiving payoffs, who did nothing but look the other way, received enough to extend their meager salaries. Most of the proceeds from the logging went to the family of the businessman and politician. Of course, nothing was invested in park management or reforestation.

Although the Isarog shrew-rat has little if any direct economic value, it and the other mammals, birds, and plants on the mountain are all part of the rain-forest ecosystem that provides a huge benefit to Naga City and the surrounding areas. The rain forest ensures a supply of clean water, protects low-lying areas from flooding during typhoons, and provides wild game, medicinal plants, recreation, and ecotourism.

The threat to the rain forest on Mount Isarog is both tragic and severe. Our studies in the park demonstrated that 27 species of birds found in the park by Professor Rabor's field team in 1961 had become locally extinct by 1988—20 percent of 135 species. All of these locally extinct species are among the 64 that live (or lived) in lowland rain forest. The Isarog shrew-rat and two other species of mammals that are known only from Mount Isarog are now listed as endangered in the *Red Data Book* of the IUCN (International Union for Conservation of Nature). On December 5, 1993, a typhoon passing through the area of Mount Isarog caused a major flood in Naga City, the first in its 420-year history. Water up to two meters deep filled the main downtown area along the Bicol River. Branches and pieces of trunks of rain-forest trees created logjams that caught parts of houses and dead domestic animals. Several people were killed, and damage to homes, businesses, agricultural fields, roads, and bridges was tremendous. The newspapers quickly pinpointed illegal logging in the vicinity of Mount Isarog as the source of the problem,

On days when the wind was still we were serenaded from dawn to dusk by the roar of chain saws and the crashing of trees echoing from lower on the slopes.

5

In 1993, deforestation produced the first major flood in the 420-year history of Naga City, depositing a thick layer of mud formed from soil that had washed off steep mountain slopes.

and highlighted the failure of protection and reforestation programs.

This story has been repeated all across the Philippines in recent years. Floods, droughts, and the siltation of coral reefs have risen dramatically as the last remnants of rain forest come under increasing pressure.

Once overlooked as a center of biological diversity, this nation of islands has now vaulted to the top of the list of "megadiversity" countries. More than 510 species of mammals, birds, frogs, and lizards have been found that are unique to the Philippines. Unfortunately, with the discovery of the richness of Philippine biodiversity has come the realization that nearly half of the unique mammals and birds are endangered. Acre-for-acre, the Philippines may have the most seriously threatened flora and fauna on earth. It is tragic that the biodiversity of the Philippines and the threat of its impending loss have been discovered simultaneously. Many and perhaps most of the species unique to the islands may become extinct before we learn that the welfare of the Philippines depends on their continued existence.

This book is a celebration of the wonderful natural diversity of this country, exploring how it developed and why it is now in such severe trouble. It is intended as a call for action not just to save the native plants and animals, but to protect the rain-forest habitat on which the Filipino people also depend for their economic and social well-being.

ISLANDS RISING

For a first-time visitor, the Philippine Islands are best approached from the sea, the same way the first humans, and most of the plants and animals, reached the archipelago. Looking toward the islands from far away, one first sees high, puffy white clouds that begin as wisps in the morning and often build to huge thunderheads by afternoon. Beneath the towering clouds appear dark outlines of islands that take on a shade of deep jade in bright tropical sunlight. The size and height of each island influence these cloud masses, and with a bit of practice it is possible to judge the size of the island—and the number of islands in the area—by gauging the size and placement of the clouds.

As one nears the islands, low, rugged mountains punctuated by high volcanoes dominate the horizon. In many places, the mountains rise quickly from the sea; in others, fertile plains of weathered volcanic soil ring the island, often covered by bright-green crops of rice and sugar cane, generously watered by the streams that flow from the wet forest on the mountains that form each island's core. From the coast well up onto the bases of the mountains grows

From far away, islands are often first visible because of the towering thunderheads that develop as humid air rises over mountains.

lowland rain forest bursting with vitality, with trees reaching over 50 meters in height. The deepest shades of green can be seen on the highest peaks, where heavy rains and cool temperatures lead to the growth of dwarf mossy forest. Animals unfamiliar to nearly all outsiders (and to most Filipinos) move quickly through the forest, on the ground and in the air; at elevations low or high, bird song fills the day and frog calls fill the night. As many as 33 typhoons may pass through the archipelago in a year, providing the water that nurtures the rain forest.

Entirely surrounded by tropical seas, the Philippine Islands are isolated from the Asian landmass by hundreds of kilometers of open water in most directions. Geological evidence now makes it clear that, with only one exception (the Palawan region), this isolation has always existed. Beginning more than 50 million years ago, the islands arose as volcanoes from the depths of the Pacific Ocean as part of the famous "Ring of Fire" that encircles most of the Pacific. Slowly drifting closer to the Asian mainland and gradually increasing in size, the Philippine archipelago has been and remains one of the most geologically active places on the

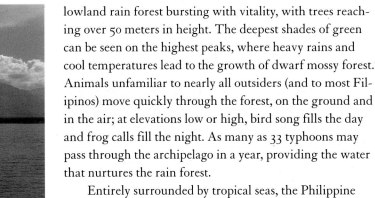

Mountainous slopes were all draped in rain forest when people first arrived in the Philippines from the Asian mainland. Outrigger canoes (RIGHT FOREGROUND) **were the primary means of inter-island transportation for hundreds and perhaps thousands of years.**

Volcanic peaks dominate the horizon in much of the country, with sulphuric fumaroles attesting to the underlying geological activity. (TOP TO BOTTOM) **Cuernos de Negros above Dumaguete City, sulphur vents on Biliran Island, and Mayon Volcano from Legaspi.**

7

The barred rail (LEFT)
and variable dwarf-
kingfisher are among
the 172 species of
birds that live only
in the Philippines.

planet. At least 17 of its volcanoes are now active, and dozens of others are considered inactive—including, until a few years ago, Mount Pinatubo, which erupted with destructive force in 1991. As a result of this volcanic history, the Philippines is one of the most fertile and mountainous countries in the world.

This history of geological isolation and gradual approach to the Asian mainland has had an enormous impact on the country's biological diversity. Birds, bats, butterflies, and other flying animals and wind-dispersed plants were able, in many cases, to surmount the difficulties of crossing broad water channels, but even for these creatures it was a rare and treacherous journey. Travel from the Asian mainland to the Philippines was so infrequent that 172 out of 395 (44 percent) of the land-birds present are found only in the Philippines. This genetic isolation could not have taken place if even a single individual of the ancestral population had flown in from the mainland just once per generation.

Among Philippine mammals

One of the 163
species of reptiles
that are unique to
the Philippines is the
anglehead lizard.

Philippine tarsiers live only on islands that were part of Ice-Age Greater Mindanao.

It is reasonable to think of the Philippines as the Galapagos Islands multiplied tenfold. More than 510 species of land mammals, birds, reptiles, and amphibians exist only in the Philippines.

that cannot fly, an amazingly high 85 percent (86 out of 101) live only in the Philippines. Many of the species that did manage to undertake the difficult journey have undergone the same kind of astounding diversification that most people associate with the Galapagos and Hawaiian Islands —a single ancestor giving rise to five, ten, or 25 descendent species, all having arisen within the Philippines. In fact, as a gauge of biological diversity, it is reasonable to think of the Philippines as the Galapagos Islands multiplied tenfold. We now estimate that more than 510 species of land-living mammals, birds, reptiles, and amphibians exist only in the Philippines. As a point of comparison, only seven of the 30 countries in Europe have *any* unique species of these groups, and the one with the highest number, Spain, has only 25 in total. Brazil, often referred to as the "storehouse of biological diversity," has about 725 unique species, about two-thirds more than the Philippines—but Brazil is 28

times larger. Madagascar, which is famous for its biological diversity, has fewer species of unique mammals than the Philippines (about 90 versus 111), despite the fact that Madagascar has *twice* the land area of the Philippines. Madagascar has the unique and remarkable lemurs that attract much attention, but the Philippines can boast of the Philippine eagle (second-largest eagle in the world), the dwarf water buffalo of Mindoro, spectacular orchids, flying lemurs, huge hornbills, and many other extraordinary species.

TERRESTRIAL VERTEBRATE FAUNA

	Total Species	Endemic Species	% Endemic
Land Mammals	174	111	64%
Breeding Land Birds	395	172	44%
Reptiles	244	163	68%
Amphibians	~85	~66	~78%
TOTAL	898	512	57%

Rugged peaks are surrounded by a narrow strip of rich farmland on Sibuyan Island.

A small fruit bat and a forest rat are among the five species of mammals unique to Sibuyan, more unique species than are found in any country in Europe.

WHY ARE THERE SO MANY SPECIES?

In 1989, our team of American and Filipino biologists briefly visited Sibuyan Island, which lies near the center of the Philippines. Even for the generally mountainous Philippines, Sibuyan is a rugged place, with a saw-toothed peak that dominates the view from nearly every point. It is small, only 463 square kilometers. Although the soil in the flat lowlands is rich, the lowlands form a narrow ring around the mountain, and the deep waters surrounding the island, although productive, are not rich enough to feed the ever-growing population. The island's inhabitants are poor, and economic opportunities for them have been few. They laughingly say that their primary export is people, and until recently the island received little attention from outsiders.

Most of the island consists of steep hillsides where most crops grow very poorly, and so the lower slopes have been planted with coconut. The upper slopes, with their original cover of rain forest, had been slowly and illegally deforested, with most of the lumber going to an adjacent island for use in several large mines. Flooding during typhoon season had been gradually increasing, as had droughts during the dry season. A pattern of increasing poverty seemed to be in place.

We had worked only a few days in the island's rain forest when, amazingly, we discovered a new species of small fruit bat, and a second trip a few years later produced four more species of small mammals that had never before been

seen by a biologist—new species that were unknown to all but a few of the local people. Although all the animals are small, and none has any special economic value, they are evidence that Sibuyan is a "center of endemism," a place that supports the world's only populations of a series of species. Finding five new, unique species of mammals on such a small island was astonishing—no other island of this size anywhere in the world is known to have so many.

Subsequently we learned that Sibuyan harbors several unique species of flowering plants, including an orchid, a palm, and a ginger plant. The beetles and lizards of Sibuyan have yet to be studied, but it would be a good bet that more new species remain to be discovered by biologists; where one or two groups show concentrations, other groups are likely to do the same.

In recognition of the need for both watershed and wildlife protection, the mountains of Sibuyan now form the core of one of the newest national parks in the country, officially designated in 1996. Almost all of the logging has ceased, giving hope that the floods and droughts will abate. An internationally supported program is developing alternative means of livelihood for the people of the island, giving them greater hope for the future. Environmental stability and survival are within reach for both people and wildlife.

But *why* are there so many unique species on Sibuyan? What quirk of nature has given it more unique species of mammals than any country in Europe? The answer lies in the unusual geological history of the Philippines.

Every Ice-Age
island is a
unique center
of diversity,
almost a world
unto itself.

The Origins and Dimensions of Biodiversity in the Philippines

LAWRENCE R. HEANEY

ANCIENT GEOLOGICAL HISTORY OF THE PHILIPPINES

Recent evidence, primarily from exploration for oil deposits, shows that the main landmass of the Philippines originated more than 50 million years ago as a series of "island arcs" far out in the Pacific Ocean. As the rocks beneath the sea were gradually squeezed between the Asian continent and the northward-moving Australian continent, which was then much farther south than it is today, parts of the sea-floor were uplifted, and others were thrust beneath the crust of the earth. The pressure and friction generated by this plate-tectonic movement produced undersea volcanoes that gradually rose above the waves. By about 30 million years ago some small but permanent islands protruded above sea level, and by 25 million years ago, several islands of at least 1,000 square kilometers had been established.

Australia continued to move northward and westward, with the pressure on the region between it and Asia forcing the precursors to the Philippine Islands to move toward Asia, resulting in still more volcanic activity. By 15 million years ago, this led to the creation of a large island of 25,000 to 50,000 square kilometers, with extensive highlands that included parts of what is presently northern Luzon. The modern southern Philippines still lay far to the south at this point, and included only a few, much smaller islands.

Southeast Asia assumed much of its current shape only about five million years ago. By this time, the modern highlands of northern Luzon were well-established. Another island reached from southern Luzon nearly to Mindanao,

and Mindanao itself consisted of several separate islands that progressively merged. Small islands continued to appear throughout the archipelago, including the Sulu Islands. Palawan and Mindoro, the only parts of the Philippines that had originated as pieces of the Asian mainland, became isolated at this time as well, with Mindoro probably dropping entirely below sea level for a time.

Although many of the details in this story remain unclear, the broad picture has become evident for the first time. We now believe that the ancient geological history of the Philippines is largely responsible for its exceptional array of biological diversity. Because the islands arose many millions of years ago, independently of the Asian mainland, with the exception of Palawan and Mindoro, they have had adequate time and space to receive and shelter rare, over-water animal and plant pioneers. But why, in comparison to nearby countries with similar climates, are levels of diversity so high in the Philippines? And why do such small islands as Sibuyan have such extraordinary numbers of unique species, while some other islands of the same size in the Philippines have none? To answer these questions, we must turn to the more recent geological history of the archipelago.

ICE-AGE HISTORY OF THE PHILIPPINES

The number of islands strewn across Southeast Asia— the region extending from the eastern edge of India to the western and northern edges of Australia and New Guinea—is astonishing. In the Philippines alone there are more than 7,000 islands, and Indonesia claims more than

12,000. One might believe, given the difficulty of movement between islands, that virtually every island would have a large number of unique species, especially among small rodents and frogs and those plants whose seeds cannot tolerate sea-water.

Although this might seem to be a good prediction, it would nevertheless be wrong. The community of mammals in the mature lowland rain forest of northern Samar, for example, barely differs from that found in the same habitat on Basilan Island, 700 kilometers away. But on Borneo, only 340 kilometers away, identical habitats are radically different, sharing only 10 percent of the mammal species on Basilan. Even more remarkable, if we compare the mammals at the northern tip of Samar with those at the southern tip of Luzon—a distance of only about 25 kilometers —we find that 80 percent of the species are different. Similar discrepancies in faunas are evident between Luzon and the adjacent island of Mindoro, and between Bohol and neighboring Negros. And Sibuyan has its own remarkable set of unique species, as does the even smaller island of Camiguin (265 square kilometers, with at least two unique small mammals and a frog), which lies only eight kilometers from the coast of Mindanao.

On the other hand, equally unexpected patterns emerge showing great similarity between faunas. The fauna on Bohol is almost identical to that on Basilan, Mindanao, Leyte, and Samar, but not to that of nearby Negros; Masbate's fauna is far more similar to Panay's than to Luzon's; and the fauna of Palawan is more similar to Borneo's than it is to that of any other island in the Philippines.

The Mindanao tree shrew (ABOVE) and northern giant cloud rat (LEFT) are members of the Greater Mindanao and Greater Luzon mammal faunas respectively, each of which contains more than 20 unique species of small mammals, as well as dozens of unique birds, frogs, and lizards, and hundreds of unique plants.

It would seem that the surface of the modern sea is hiding some underlying patterns.

The explanation for these patterns of similarity and dissimilarity may be found in an event—actually, a repeated series of events—that may be familiar to those of us who live in North America and Europe. Fifteen- to twenty- thousand years ago, the regions now occupied by Chicago, St. Paul, Toronto, and many other North Ameri-

ICE-AGE S. E. ASIA

During the recent Ice Age, sea level dropped to about 120 meters below the present level, exposing huge areas as dry land, but the Philippines remained isolated by deep channels. The former riverbeds are still visible on the shallow sea-floor between Borneo and Java, Sumatra, and the Malay Peninsula.

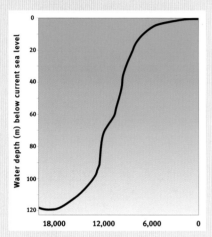

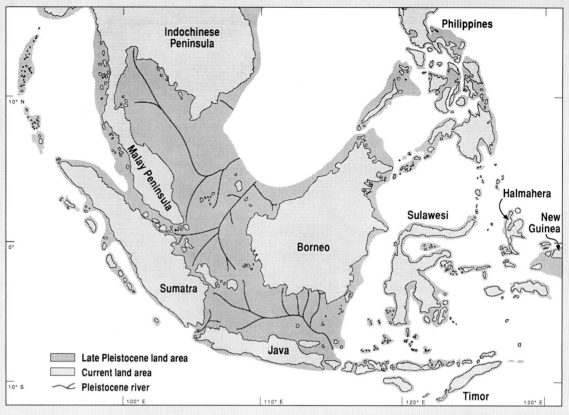

Late Pleistocene land area
Current land area
Pleistocene river

Source: Heaney 1991; Fairbanks, 1989.

can cities, and by London, Copenhagen, and Moscow in Europe, were covered by sheets of ice more than a kilometer thick. These huge continental glaciers form about every 140,000 years, gradually growing and melting as the result of subtle shifts in the orbit of the earth around the sun. We now know that glaciers appeared at least 21 different times over the past several million years. This period of alternating glacial growth and melting is generally known as the Ice Age, or, more technically, as the Pleistocene Epoch.

The glaciers formed after water evaporating from the oceans was deposited on land as snow. In years when more snow fell in winter than could melt in summer, the glaciers grew. As the snow piled higher, the lower layers were compacted into ice by the weight from above. The existence of that ice—enough to cover nearly all of the northern half of North America and large parts of northern Europe and Asia, as well as some other regions—had a huge impact on

the oceans, since water that stayed on the continents in the form of ice and snow was equaled by a drop in sea level. When the ice sheets were at their peak in the most recent phase of glacial growth (15,000 to 20,000 years ago), sea level was 120 meters (400 feet) lower than it is today.

In Southeast Asia, where some seas are rather shallow —often less than 80 meters deep—the impact of this change in sea level was enormous. Borneo, Java, and Sumatra were merged with the Asian continent in a great peninsula, much of it a broad, fertile lowland plain. Huge rivers flowed across this plain, leaving behind channels so deep and prominent that they can still be seen on the floor of the South China and Java seas, up to 80 meters below the current sea level. Freshwater fish found in streams in northern Java are most closely related to those in streams on southern Borneo, evidence of the freshwater rivers that once flowed across what is now the Java Sea.

14

Around the edge of that giant Asian peninsula, water depths were (and are still) much greater—hundreds to thousands of meters—and so these areas remained permanently as sea. Some islands merged to form larger but still isolated landmasses, while other islands grew somewhat but remained minimally affected.

The reasons for the odd patterns of distribution and diversity in the region now become clear. Land mammal faunas in northern Samar and Basilan are so similar because the animals were able to walk on dry land from one of these sites to the other. To go from northern Samar to the adjacent tip of Luzon, however, would have required that they cross a sea channel about ten kilometers wide. Mammals, frogs, and plants are able to spread across places with continuous habitat, even when thousands of kilometers are involved, but have great difficulty crossing even ten kilometers of sea water. The repercussions of this land distribution on biological diversity in Southeast Asia, the "land of islands," were enormous.

We now know that in the Philippines, faunal regions —the natural units of biodiversity—were determined largely by the configuration of the Ice-Age islands. We can map these configurations easily by drawing the shoreline as it existed about 20,000 years ago, when the seas were 120 meters below their present level. (The ancient beaches are still visible on the sea floor in some places.) An entirely new image of the Philippines then emerges: an Ice-Age island of Greater Luzon in the north that included several adjacent smaller islands; an island of Greater Mindanao in the south that included Leyte, Bohol, Samar, and many other smaller islands; and an island of Greater Negros-Panay in the center that merged Cebu, Masbate, Negros, and Panay. Dozens of other islands harbored their own unique sets of species in their rain forests. As best we can tell, each of these islands remained permanently isolated from the others. The image of the Philippines being composed of many distinctive sets of islands thus becomes even more robust, and the description of the Philippines as "the Galapagos Islands times ten" becomes even more apt. Every Ice-Age island in the Philippines is a unique center of diversity, even those only 250 square kilometers in area.

And so we see that roughly 80 percent of the non-flying mammals on Greater Mindanao are found nowhere

ICE-AGE ISLANDS OF THE PHILIPPINES

Redrawn from Heaney 1986, 1991.

During the most recent Ice Age, when sea level was 120 meters lower than at present, land bridges formed between many islands in the Philippines, although many deep channels remained. Each of the Ice-Age islands (Sibuyan and Greater Negros-Panay are examples) has a unique set of species of plants and animals.

white stripes, small shrew-like rodents, and a wide range of equally unfamiliar animals. At least 70 percent of the non-flying mammals on Greater Luzon are found nowhere else. Because they have been isolated from one another, each of the Ice-Age islands has its own set of strange but appealing creatures: On Greater Palawan, 48 percent of the mammals are unique; on Greater Mindoro, 44 percent; and on Greater Negros-Panay, 50 percent. For frogs, lizards, bats, birds, trees, and orchids, the story is much the same—enormous diversity composed of many isolated sets of species, each of the Ice-Age islands almost a world unto itself.

CLIMATE AND BIODIVERSITY

Temperature, on average, declines with increases in elevation. Baguio City, for example, often called the "summer capital of the Philippines," was chosen as a refuge from the summer heat of Manila because it lies 1,524 meters above sea level in the Central Cordillera. When air blows uphill, it gradually expands due to the slow decline in pressure (resulting from the reduced weight of the air above it in the atmosphere). As the air expands, it cools at a rate determined by its water content; air that is saturated with water cools more slowly than dry air. In the Philippines, where air is almost always humid, air cools at an average rate of 6° Centigrade for every 1,000 meters that it rises. On a hot, muggy day in Manila, when the temperature is a sizzling 34° C (93° Fahrenheit), it will typically be 25° C (77° F) in Baguio. Still higher in the mountains—for example, near the top of Mount Pulog, north of Baguio at nearly 3,000 meters elevation—the temperature will typically be only 16° C (61° F).

Along with the change in temperature comes a change in precipitation. As air cools, it gradually loses its ability to hold humidity; when it reaches its saturation point, water molecules begin to gather in tiny droplets and form clouds. Clouds often produce rain, but they also become fog when they encounter the top of a mountain. As a result, rainfall (and dew-fall) usually increases as we go up any given mountain. The lowlands of the Philippines experience roughly two meters of rain annually, but at 900 meters elevation (about 3,000 feet), rainfall is approximately two and a half times higher. Farther up in the mountains, at about

Clouds often form over mountains, dropping up to five times as much rain as in the lowlands.

else in the world. These unique species include such mammals as flying lemurs (odd creatures distantly related to bats), tree shrews (which may be ancient relatives of the primates), tree squirrels, and tarsiers (bug-eyed primates that eat lizards and large insects). On Greater Luzon, just a few kilometers away at its closest point, we see none of the species characteristic of Greater Mindanao. In their place we find giant cloud rats that feed on tender young leaves in the treetops, bizarre long-snouted rodents that eat almost nothing but earthworms, other rodents with black-and-

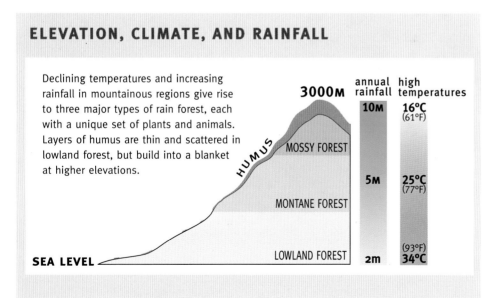

ELEVATION, CLIMATE, AND RAINFALL

Declining temperatures and increasing rainfall in mountainous regions give rise to three major types of rain forest, each with a unique set of plants and animals. Layers of humus are thin and scattered in lowland forest, but build into a blanket at higher elevations.

3000M

HUMUS

MOSSY FOREST

MONTANE FOREST

SEA LEVEL

LOWLAND FOREST

	annual rainfall	high temperatures
	10M	16°C (61°F)
	5M	25°C (77°F)
		(93°F)
	2m	34°C

2,000 meters elevation, rainfall is often five times higher than in the adjacent lowlands.

The net result of these changes in temperature and precipitation is dramatic. While daytime temperatures average 30° C in the lowlands, they rarely exceed 18° C on the mountains 2,000 meters above sea level, and while the lowlands receive two meters of rain annually (about six feet, a bit more than twice the yearly average of Chicago), the mountains may be subject to as much as 12 meters per year (about 40 feet). Lowland rain forest is wet, but mossy forest in the higher mountains is much, much wetter.

Another feature of the Philippine climate is one that every citizen of the country knows only too well: The Philippines lies at the center of the primary typhoon track in Asia. As many as 33 typhoons can strike the archipelago in a single year, with 15 to 25 being typical. These storms bring winds powerful enough to topple high-tension power lines and tear bamboo huts to shreds, and can drop half a meter of rain or more in a day.

When such heavy rain falls on rain forest, the leaves of the trees break its fall so that it lands softly on the ground, which is usually loosely covered with leaves and small plants. In high-elevation mossy forest, where rainfall is still heavier and the terrain much steeper, the cool temperatures allow the accumulation of thick layers of partially decomposed leaves, branches, and moss which function as a huge sponge. A meter of rainfall in a day in mossy forest produces remarkably little flooding; most of the moisture simply disappears into the natural sponge of humus and soil, to be gradually released from springs in the lowlands.

HABITAT AND BIODIVERSITY

Climate is largely responsible for shaping the four widespread and several restricted types of habitats that originally occurred in the Philippines.

Originally the most common type of habitat, tropical lowland rain forest best fits the popular image of rain forest. The largest trees—two to three meters in diameter, not counting the massive supporting buttresses—reach 30 to 40 meters into the canopy, and a few stretch to 60 meters in height. Many of these trees belong to a single family, the dipterocarps, known for the beautifully lustrous wood

marketed as "Philippine mahogany." Lianas and other vines reach from the ground to the canopy, providing a natural highway on which monkeys, squirrels, civet-cats, and lizards move from the dark quiet of the forest floor to the sunlight far above. Huge strangler fig trees wrap their tendrils around the branches and trunks of other trees, gradually overwhelming and killing their hosts, but the fig fruit they produce provides much of the food for raucous parrots, giant fruit bats, monkeys, and dozens of insect species. High in the canopy, delicate orchids and ferns grow in profusion, creating small pockets of soil dozens of meters above

Many trees in lowland tropical rain forest have tall, straight trunks, especially the dipterocarps (LEFT) **that are marketed as Philippine mahogany.**

Strangler figs (ABOVE) **are common in tropical lowland forests, producing food for dozens of species of birds and mammals. Huge buttresses** (ABOVE RIGHT) **support the trunks of larger trees.**

ground where tiny communities of earthworms, springtails, geckoes, and other species thrive. Surprisingly, the soil on the forest floor is often very thin and rocky because the high temperatures and wet conditions allow for extremely rapid decomposition of leaves and wood. Temperatures in lowland rain forest almost always remain high, and a breath of wind is as rare on the forest floor as it is ubiquitous in the canopy above. Humidity within the forest rarely drops below 90 percent, even when weeks pass between rainstorms. In a few parts of the Philippines, the dry season lasts long enough that some trees drop their leaves for several months, but in most places the forest remains green and vibrant throughout the year.

Beginning at about 1,000 meters elevation on most mountains, but starting as high as 1,700 meters on the highest and largest mountains, the lowland forest grades into montane forest. Montane forest is shorter, reaching only to about 15 to 20 meters, with a maximum of 25 meters, and the trees rarely have the buttresses that are so conspicuous at lower elevation. Trees in the oak and laurel families dominate; vines are even more abundant, including an

Montane forest on steep mountainsides, such as that surrounding Lake Balinsasayao on Negros Island, receives more than twice the rainfall of lowland forest.

Vines, including pitcher plants (ABOVE), **thrive in montane forest** (RIGHT), **as do sunbirds** (BELOW), **which feed on nectar from flowers.**

odd viney member of the palm group called pandans *(Freycinetia)* that is often festooned over the large trees. Pitcher plants and orchids are increasingly abundant in the trees; on the ground, moss covers roots and tree trunks, and leaf-litter covers rich organic soil. Rainfall here is high—two to three times that at sea level—and falls through most of the year, leaving the forest dripping with water. Sunbirds, resplendent with metallic greens, blues, and reds, flit through the trees seeking nectar from flowers, and, on the southern islands, giant flying squirrels chatter noisily in the night.

Still higher in the mountains, montane forest gradually gives way to mossy forest (sometimes called upper montane forest), in many ways the most dramatic and mysterious forest in the Philippines. Rainfall here may be the highest in the world—our site near the top of Mount Isarog, in southern Luzon near Naga City, gets up to 12 meters of rain per year; this is almost ten times the amount that falls in Portland, Oregon, famous for its damp climate, and five times more than the rainfall in Naga City near sea level.

Mossy forest is a miniature world of deep jade green, where a startling array of orchids, ferns, and mosses can grow on a single rotting log.

During most of the year, clouds flow into the forest at the tops of the mountains, saturating the long strands of moss that hang from the trees and causing up to several centimeters of drip-fall on nights when, technically, no rain has fallen. Because temperatures here are quite cool (averaging just 18° C for daily high temperature) and rainfall is so high, plants grow in thick profusion. High winds and steep terrain also work to keep trees small (only two to six meters), and nearly all trees are twisted and gnarled, looking much like a fairytale elfin forest. It is a miniature world of deep jade green, where a startling array of orchids, ferns, and mosses can grow on a single rotting log. Leaves, roots, moss, and branches decay more slowly than they are produced in a mossy forest, so that huge, springy mats of partially decayed vegetation, held together by live roots, can build to four or five meters deep. Open spaces within the mats provide a matrix of soil, caverns, and tunnel-ways for dense populations of earthworms, rodents, and poorly known frogs. It is this habitat that has, proportionately, the highest numbers of unique species; on Mount Kitanglad, in northern Mindanao, a recent survey found that all twelve of the small mammals present, including two previously unknown species, were unique to the Philippines. All 16 of the bird species native only to Mindanao were abundant as well, including such remarkable species as the Apo mynah, the Apo sunbird, and the parrot-finch. Perhaps most startlingly, all ten of the species of earthworms found there were previously unknown to biologists.

Mossy forest, with its cool, wet climate, has the highest proportion of unique species of any habitat in the Philippines.

In a few parts of the country that lie moderately far from the sea and within the rain-shadow of other mountains, another type of forest flourishes at 900 to 1,500 meters elevation—pine forest. This habitat is dominated by two species of pines also found to the north and west in Asia *(Pinus insularis* and *P. merkusii)*. The longer-than-average dry seasons in these parts of the country promote fairly frequent fires that kill other trees but are tolerated by the pines; the resulting habitat is a parkland with pine trees widely separated by grassy areas. Heavy rains fall during parts of the year, and fog can be common. These regions are home not only to the world-famous rice terraces of the Ifugao and Bontoc people, but also to several birds familiar to northerners—crossbills and bullfinches—and to an exceptionally odd but beautiful rodent the size of a large house-cat, with long, flowing, silky black hair, known as the Luzon bushy-tailed cloud rat.

Three additional types of habitat deserve mention, even though they originally occupied only a small portion of the country (and even less today). Mangrove forest can be found in coastal areas where sea water and fresh water mixed in bays and at the mouths of rivers. Due to the influx of organic material carried by the rivers, biological productivity in such places is very high. Mangrove forest is a crucial breeding habitat for many species of marine fish and shore birds.

Pine forest (ABOVE) **and mangrove forest** (BELOW) **are geographically restricted habitats that add significantly to overall diversity in the Philippines.**

Each of these forest habitats possesses individual climatic features that enable a unique set of plants and animals to survive.

Limestone (LEFT) **and ultrabasic forest** (BELOW) **occur only where there are unusual soil conditions.**

In places where limestone outcrops cover extensive areas, natural erosion has given rise to a beautiful landscape referred to as "karst," dominated by white cliffs and ridges riddled with small caves. Rainwater quickly drains away into the caves, leaving behind parched conditions where only a few species of trees can prosper. The forest here, usually called limestone forest, is dominated by the molave tree (*Vitex parviflora*), which tends to grow in the few pockets of deep soil, with clumps of bamboo and small leguminous trees occupying much of the remaining land. The diversity of plants here is low, but those plants that are present tend to be highly restricted, unique species that provide habitat for a unique set of butterflies and other insects.

The final type of forest forms where unusual rocks, called ultrabasic or serpentines, predominate. The soils that form from these rocks are extremely unproductive because they are very high in iron and magnesium and very low in most other nutrients, allowing only specialized species of plants to survive. The ultrabasic forest thus supports only a few species, although many of those are restricted to the Philippines. It is often low in stature, giving rise in some places to a shrubby, heath-like vegetation.

Each of these forest habitats contributes to the grand structure of the natural environment of the Philippines, and possesses individual climatic features that enable a unique set of plants and animals to survive. All of these habitats may be present in one form or another on all of the Ice-Age islands described above. Diversity in the Philippines is therefore determined not just geographically, but also climatically within each island. It is the combination of geological and climatic variation that has led to the profusion of life in the Philippines, a profusion not of large numbers of species residing in a single vast habitat, as in the Amazon basin, but of sets of species unique to a great number of small areas of habitat. The diversity of life indigenous to the Philippines is a story of unique places, each with its own tale to tell.

Vanishing Treasures

JACINTO C. REGALADO, JR. AND LAWRENCE R. HEANEY

GOLDEN-CROWNED FLYING FOX

AS THE LATE AFTERNOON SUN drops over the Sierra Madre mountains in northeastern Luzon, a group of huge trees nearly bare of leaves but supporting what seem to be very large, dark, oblong fruit undergoes a rapid and strange transformation. The "fruit," which have been swaying and shifting despite the absence of a breeze, give a shake and abruptly open huge wings. Hundreds, then thousands, then tens of thousands of bats begin to stretch, greeting their neighbors with harsh, squawking calls and clambering around the trees to their favorite spots for taking flight. With wingspans of five feet or more, and weighing 1,200 grams or more (about three pounds), these golden-crowned flying foxes (*Acerodon jubatus*) are probably the heaviest bats in the world. Living among them is another, similar species of large flying fox (*Pteropus vampyrus*), which weighs less but has an even greater wingspan. The entire group together numbers perhaps 50,000 bats, which fly off in all directions in search of fruit. They may fly 40 kilometers or more each night looking for ripe figs, their favorite food.

Prior to World War I, colonies of giant fruit bats numbering from 50,000 to 150,000 were reported on every large island in the country. The largest islands had many such colonies; a reasonable guess for Mindanao would be more than 20, for a total of at least two million giant bats. These bats were an integral part of the lowland rain forest; the seeds in the fruit they ate traveled quickly through their digestive tracts, and were voided as they flew. The rain of seeds (complete with fertilizer) from the giant bats overhead was critical in maintaining ecological stability, since fig trees—whose seedlings can tolerate the harsh tropical sun—are central to recolonizing land laid bare by fire, landslide, or volcanic eruption.

The golden-crowned flying fox (RIGHT, AT CENTER) **originally lived in colonies of over 100,000 individuals. Their slow, steady wingbeats can carry them at least 40 kilometers in a night.**

By the mid-1980s, widespread destruction of lowland rain forest had reduced the bats' habitat to a fraction of its original extent. The bats also were subject to heavy hunting by impoverished subsistence farmers. Most colonies had disappeared entirely, and those known to still persist were down to a few thousand individuals at best, often only a few hundred. Survival seemed tenuous. But in the mid-1990s, researchers in the Sierra Madre wilderness found a new colony of 50,000 to 60,000 giant fruit bats—the best hope for the survival of one of the most remarkable mammals on earth.

STRANGLER FIGS

STRANGLER FIGS *(Ficus)* begin life as a small seed deposited by a bird, fruit bat, or other animal on the branches of a canopy tree. At first it is a harmless little epiphyte (see page 32). Soon it begins to send its branches upward and its roots downward. From that moment on, the giant tree on which the strangler lives is doomed. Quickly, the strangler's roots compete with those of the host tree for water and nutrients. They have an extraordinary ability to fuse and form a mesh around the host tree, which eventually dies from being deprived of sunlight and nutrients. In its place will stand a giant fig tree, upon which will occur one of the most complex partnerships in nature.

Strangler figs produce three kinds of very small flowers that may be found in varying combinations lining the inner surface of its hollow, ovoid pseudo-fruits called figs: male flowers producing only pollen; female flowers with long styles and fertile ovaries; and gall flowers with short styles and infertile ovaries. The narrow openings of the figs attract female wasps, which, loaded with pollen, will enter and try to lay their eggs. If a wasp enters a "gall fig" containing male and gall flowers, she will lay her eggs in each of the ovaries of the gall flowers. If she enters a fig with only female flowers, she will try to deposit her eggs on the ovaries but will fail because the styles are too long for her ovipositor to reach them. On the other hand, these wasps do brush pollen onto the fertile ovaries, which then set seeds. Meanwhile, in the gall flowers, the wasp's offspring emerge. Inside the fig, the small, wingless male wasps will copulate with the winged females, then die, never having left the fig. At this time the male flowers ripen and shed pollen onto the young female wasps, which exit to search for a new place to lay their eggs. (If there are birds swarming over a fig tree, that's a sure sign the wasps are emerging from their hideaways.) After a while, the fruits will ripen, turning from green to red and becoming a delicious feast for hungry birds and mammals. The animals will then pass the fertilized seeds undamaged through their intestines, thus completing the cycle.

Strangler figs are often huge, dwarfing a human in the forest. Their fruits, which frequently grow directly from branches and even the trunk, are a critical food resource for dozens of species.

Soon the little plant begins to send its branches upward and its roots downward. From that moment on, the giant tree on which the strangler lives is doomed.

FLAME-BREASTED FRUIT DOVE

Flame-breasted fruit doves can survive only in the old-growth forests of central and northern Luzon.

PIGEONS AND DOVES ARE FAMILIAR to almost everyone as adaptable animals that thrive in our city parks. Although breeders have produced some fancy varieties of domestic pigeons, all are colored in shades of gray, white, and brown, with only hints of iridescent color. This image leaves most of us poorly prepared for the flame-breasted fruit dove of Luzon. One of 33 species of pigeons and doves in the Philippines (16 of which occur nowhere else in the world), this spectacular bird has a large patch of bright orange vermilion in the center of its chest, a cinnamon-red head, wings spotted with carmine, and crimson feet.

As the name implies, flame-breasted fruit doves *(Ptilinopus marchei)* feed on fruits and berries in the old-growth montane and mossy forest where they live. Seeds usually pass through their guts without damage, so these birds are crucial in propagating many of the forest's unique plant species. These doves live only in very small groups (probably just a pair), and lay a single egg each time they nest.

Since flame-breasted fruit doves can survive only in their native old-growth forest habitat in the central and northern parts of Luzon, they have been hard-hit by deforestation. As one of the largest doves in the Philippines (reaching 16 inches from the tip of the bill to the tip of the tail) it has been the object of persistent over-hunting (both by shooting and by placing sticky lime on branches of trees where the doves roost). Fortunately, a large enough population of doves inhabits the mountains in the new Northern Sierra Madre Wilderness Park to sustain itself in that area. Elsewhere, their populations continue to shrink steadily.

Some other unique Philippine doves have not been so lucky. Three species of bleeding-heart pigeons from Negros, Mindoro, and Sulu—so named for the small patches of bright crimson feathers on their breasts—are among the most severely endangered doves in the world. Six additional species are also endangered, and one species is feared to be extinct.

Flame-breasted fruit doves (TOP) **are the most beautiful of the 33 species of pigeons and doves in the Philippines, 16 of which are found nowhere else. The Mindoro imperial-pigeon** (BOTTOM) **is seriously endangered by habitat destruction and the Negros fruit-dove** (RIGHT) **may be extinct.**

SLENDER-TAILED CLOUD RATS

RATS AND MICE have a bad reputation. The very word "rat" in English immediately brings to mind a squinty-eyed, ugly, voracious, disease-ridden, aggressive animal that breeds prolifically unless constantly opposed through trapping and poisoning. There are, of course, such animals, and we all know them only too well. But most rat and mouse species are well-mannered, clean, rather pretty, and shy, and pose no threat to humans. Of the 63 species of rats and mice in the Philippines, only six are responsible for causing more than very minor damage to anything, and those six were all accidentally imported from the Asian mainland and are not native to the Philippines. Each of the native species is an important part of the food-web that binds together the rain-forest biological community. They range from such small and surprising species as the Isarog shrew-rat (mentioned at the beginning of this book) to such large and startling species as the slender-tailed cloud rats.

Weighing up to two and a half kilograms, the northern slender-tailed cloud rats *(Phloeomys pallidus)* are the largest "rats" in the world, using the taxonomic rather than the popular definition of a rat. But few people would recognize them as rats; most Americans and Filipinos might guess from their long, furry tails, large eyes, and quiet disposition that they are strange squirrels. The color pattern of one of the two known species of this rat, though, is different from any squirrel's: The species from central and northern Luzon is mostly covered in nearly white fur, with dark ears, a dark tail, and a dark brown mask around the eyes, nose, and mouth. Some populations have a brown cape over the shoulders. The species from southern Luzon *(Phloeomys cumingi)* is a deep mahogany brown all over; a group of related species, the bushy-tailed cloud rats (the genus *Crateromys*), includes one species with long, flowing, coal-black hair that covers the entire body, and another that is bright orange over most of the body, but with a tail that is pure white for the last half of its length.

As far as we know, all of the cloud rats feed on tender young leaves in trees that grow in lowland rain forest. They are slow-moving and seem to spend a great deal of time digesting their latest meal. In a large hollow tree or log, the females give birth to one young per year, which stays with the mother (the father hangs around only for mating) until the next young is born a year later. At one time, they were probably the primary prey for bird and mammal carnivores over much of the Philippines, possibly including the Philippine eagle in the Sierra Madre Mountains, where both the eagle and cloud rat were common until the end of World War II.

Because they are large and meaty, the cloud rats are all heavily hunted; one subsistence farmer living at the base of Mount Isarog told us that he used his dogs to track and kill 50 per year. The combination of heavy hunting and habitat destruction has led to one species probably having gone extinct (on Mindoro), one that is critically endangered (on Panay), and the four others being threatened to varying degrees. Ironically, the cloud rats appear to be the only native species of "rats and mice" in the Philippines that have much economic impact, either positive or negative. If the habitat of these mammals were protected and hunting effectively regulated, they could remain a welcome source of protein to poor farmers. Extinct species, however, are notoriously poor at providing any benefits.

Slender-tailed cloud rats are quiet, timid animals that weigh up to two and a half kilograms and feed on tender young leaves in the rain forest.

FROGS

Although frogs look much alike, they vary from stout, ground-dwelling animals (BELOW) to slender tree-dwelling species (RIGHT) and streamlined animals that live mostly in water (BOTTOM RIGHT).

FROGS ARE REMARKABLY DIVERSE in the Philippines —80 to 90 species are now known, about 20 of which have been discovered in just the past five years. Both facts—the large numbers and the frequent discovery of new species—may initially come as a surprise, but make sense in retrospect. Frogs are quite sensitive to salt water, and most species die quickly in sea water. Although typhoons may occasionally create rafts of vegetation on which frogs can be propelled across the ocean by strong winds, most of the time they are unable to move between islands. And so we find that most of the Ice-Age islands have a unique set of frog species, just as they do with other groups of animals and plants.

The rapid discovery of new species is explained by two recent developments. First, the number of field biologists and field projects in the Philippines has increased rapidly in the past ten years, so more information is available than ever before, especially from the poorly known montane and mossy forests. Second, as logging roads reach ever farther into previously inaccessible areas, biologists have been scrambling to get to the forest before it disappears. Ironically, biodiversity is often discovered within earshot of chain saws.

All frogs have much the same body plan, but there is considerable diversity in the details of their appearance, and an even greater variation in their reproductive biology. Although many frogs lay large numbers of eggs in small ponds, as is widely known, most species do not. Some species lay their eggs only in fast-moving mountain streams, virtually glueing them to rocks; others lay them in tree hollows and at the base of leafy stems of pandans and ferns where rainwater accumulates; still others lay their eggs in wet moss, where there is no standing water at all. Although most species develop into tadpoles before they metamorphose into adults, all of the species in the genus *Platymantis* undergo direct development—a tiny froglet climbs out of the egg, with no tadpole stage at all. Frogs that lay eggs in tree hollows and leaf axils often skip the tadpole stage and lay only five to ten large eggs; frogs that lay eggs in large ponds can produce up to 2,000 at a time.

Because many species of frogs live in streams and ponds for much of their lives, they are among the most sensitive indicators of water quality and watershed condition. Of the 80 to 90 species now known, 60 to 70 percent are threatened by habitat destruction. An unexpected source of pressure on the native species has come from the recent escape of several non-native species (from North America and mainland Asia) from commercial farms on Luzon that produce frog legs for export to other Asian countries. These non-native species are aggressively colonizing central Luzon, competing with unique native species for food.

PHILIPPINE EAGLE-OWL

LIKE SO MANY OTHER GROUPS in the Philippines, owls come in an amazing variety of sizes and habits, often with five or six species living in the same area. The smallest are only seven inches long, about the size of a large thrush such as the American robin. These little birds feed on a seemingly unlikely but abundant prey: beetles and crickets. At the other end of the scale is the Philippine eagle-owl *(Bubo philippensis)*, one of the largest owls in the world, with a wingspan of about 48 inches (120 centimeters). What the eagle-owl eats is a mystery; the species is so poorly known that not even this basic information is available. We do know, however, that most observations of the species have been made in lowland forest near or beside rivers. Since a related species in Malaysia feeds on fish, the Philippine eagle-owl might also.

The small species of owls have been conspicuous and pleasant companions to us on many nights in the Philippine forest, their clear whistling and hooting calls softly sounding in the quiet night air. Most of the small owls occur in a range of old-growth forest habitats, and some are able to survive in fairly small forest patches. Still, four small Philippine species are now vulnerable to extinction due to massive habitat destruction. The Philippine eagle-owl and the lesser eagle-owl *(Mimizuku guerneyi)* are in even worse shape because they live only in lowland forest, and their large size requires that they have large tracts of forest to maintain populations. If rivers are indeed a crucial part of their habitat, that is bad news for the owls, because old-growth forest along rivers is now especially rare. Of course, protecting habitat for the owls would also benefit the people who live downstream, since protecting forest along rivers would help control floods.

There are at least 16 species of owls in the Philippines, from the little Philippine scops-owl (RIGHT) **to the Philippine eagle-owl, one of the largest in the world** (ABOVE LEFT).

What the eagle-owl eats is a mystery; the species is so poorly known that not even this basic information is available.

JADE VINE

At their peak, the flower clusters are spectacular, but when not in flower the vine virtually disappears among its neighbors.

ONE OF THE MOST PRIZED TREASURES of the Philippine rain forest is the jade vine *(Strongylodon macrobotrys)*. A popular attraction in many conservatories and greenhouses in temperate countries, the plant was first seen in 1854 by botanists who were members of the U.S. Wilkes Exploring Expedition in the dipterocarp forest of Mount Makiling on Luzon. The common name, jade vine, refers to the rare jade or bluish-green color of its flowers. Each flower is five to seven centimeters long, boat-shaped, and

gently curved like the upturned beak of a bird. The flowers are clustered in bouquets 60 to 90 centimeters long, which hang gracefully from the stem. At their peak, the flower clusters are spectacular, but when not in flower the vine virtually disappears among its neighbors in the forest. After flowering, the vine produces large oblong fruits with short-lived seeds that remain viable for only a week or two.

Woody climbers such as the jade vine are called lianas; their abundance in tropical rain forests—they make up an estimated ten percent of the total species—paints the popular image of impenetrable jungle. Once rooted in the ground, the plant grows toward light in the canopy, twisting like a rope around the trunks and branches of tall trees. With age, the stems become tough, woody, and thick, helping to support the giant dipterocarps, which are often rooted in very thin soil. Removal of trees results in the loss of lianas, which depend reciprocally on the trees for support. While lianas seem to grow abundantly after a forest is logged, a careful inventory will show that the number of species has drastically decreased. Aggressive and weedy species from outside the forest often move in and occupy the open space, and so lianas like the jade vine have become one of the most threatened groups of plants in the Philippines.

RED-BELLIED PITTA

MORE THAN 135 SPECIES OF BIRDS have been found on Mount Isarog. Most of them (116 species) breed on the mountain and never move far from home; only 19 are migratory species that breed in the temperate zone, far to the north. The variety of these birds is dazzling—eleven species of hawks, eagles, and falcons; eleven wild pigeons and doves; five species of kingfishers; eight thrushes; two kinds of hornbills; six cuckoo-shrikes; six sunbirds; eleven cuckoos; and dozens of more and less familiar species. Some, like the hornbills, are large and raucous, and are a conspicuous element in traditional folklore; others, like the two species of pittas, are small and rarely seen.

Red-bellied pittas *(Pitta erythrogaster)* live in lowland rain forest, primarily along rivers and streams. They usually move not by flying or walking, but by taking short, careful hops across the dimly-lit forest floor in search of beetles, snails, and other small creatures to eat. Although they make brief, clear whistling calls during breeding season, they are generally silent, and usually reveal themselves only through the rustling of leaves. But a rare shaft of sunlight reaching the forest floor may illuminate a crimson breast and a flash of metallic-blue wings as a pitta quickly takes a short flight to hide again among the fallen leaves.

Many of the unique species of birds in the Philippines, including the red-bellied pitta, depend on forested areas adjacent to lowland streams and rivers, a habitat that is also crucial for watershed protection.

A rare shaft of sunlight reaching the forest floor may illuminate a crimson breast and a flash of metallic-blue wings.

LIPSTICK PLANTS

EPIPHYTES OR "AIR PLANTS" grow on other plants, frequently large trees, although they are not parasites. Their roots do not penetrate the host tree, they merely use its surface for support. In the forest canopy, epiphytes do not have to compete for space with plants that root on the ground. They are, however, limited by the availability of water and nutrients, and for this reason mostly grow in wet montane and cool cloud forests.

Among the more spectacular epiphytes are the lipstick plants *(Aeschynanthus)*, so named because of their very bright, flamboyant red flowers. Horticulturists and gardeners have been inventive in naming various species of this group of vines—from the riotous "royal red bugler" and "scarlet basket vine" to the demure and modest "blush wort" and "climbing beauty." Lipstick plants are members of the African violet and gloxinia family, known for its many popular cultivated ornamentals.

With more than 100 species in Asia, lipstick plants in the Philippines number at least 25 species, presumably all endemic to the country. They are sometimes encountered in damp primary forests at low elevations, but become more numerous in high mossy forests. In contrast to the many woody climbers in the forest, the delicate, herbaceous vines of lipstick plants twist softly around tree branches. In addition to their brilliant, flame-red tubular flowers, these beautiful epiphytes are conspicuous for their fleshy, bright green leaves. The flower tubes often resemble exaggerated lips, the broad lower lip providing a suitable landing platform for insect pollinators, particularly bees attracted to brilliant red colors. Four stamens protrude from the mouth of the flower tube. As bees enter the mouth of the tube in search of the sweet nectar at its base, they collect pollen on their backs. Each bee will carry thousands of pollen grains to the next flower it visits, fertilizing a great number of ovules that eventually turn into

seeds. Ants nesting on tree trunks and limbs presumably carry thousands of these tiny seeds to their hidden abodes, where they will germinate to form new plants.

Lipstick plants and other herbaceous plants in the understory are especially susceptible to the removal of trees that shelter them from the bright sun. We know very little about the reproductive biology of these plants; their demise would be a serious loss to science and to the horticulture industry, which depends on such knowledge for its successful cultivation and breeding methods.

Many small plants in the rain forest grow only high in the canopy, sending their roots into crevices in the bark of tree branches. The lipstick plants are examples.

MOSSES

ALTHOUGH MOSSES AND ALGAE are two distinct groups, they are referred to in Tagalog by the same general name, *lumot*. Both are small plants with little or no differentiation into roots, stems, or leaves. Because both groups lack tissues for the efficient circulation and storage of water, algae and mosses require constant moisture. The algae have easily solved this problem by remaining aquatic. The mosses have developed several adaptations that enable them to live on land, but these are not sufficient to withstand more than brief and rather minor water deficits.

In lowland forests, a limited number of moss species thrives in damp, shady areas where moisture on the ground and water vapor in the atmosphere are always available. A sudden change, however, begins at about 1,000 meters on forested mountains throughout the Philippines: Mosses uncommon on lower slopes abruptly form a luxuriant green carpet on almost everything—tree trunks, twigs and branches, rocks and fallen logs, even the surfaces of leaves. The abundance of mosses, especially above 1,700 meters, is the reason such habitats are called "mossy forest." With increasing altitude, on wind-swept slopes and ridge tops, trees in mossy forests are gnarled and only a few meters tall. Mosses festoon their branches and hang like beards, giving the whole forest an eerie feeling.

On the ground, mosses grow very close to each other, forming a dense mat or cushion that can absorb and retain great amounts of water. As new shoots grow, older ones die and are compressed underneath; eventually the layers of dead material turn into peat several meters deep. These layers of peat absorb and distribute the heavy rains on the mountains into the groundwater system and small forest streams, thus preventing disastrous floods in the lowlands.

The moss flora of the Philippines includes about 700 species, about 50 of which are unique to the country, including one endemic genus, *Merrilliobryum*. Although mosses are widespread, many species are poorly documented; much more research on these critical indicators of forest vitality is needed.

Mosses are among the most important plants in the Philippines because of the role they play in forming the soils on high mountains that absorb rain during typhoons.

PHILIPPINE DWARF FRUIT BAT

It flies at night beneath the canopy seeking out the ripe fruit of pepper plants, figs, wild bananas, and other forest plants.

IN THE LOWLAND FOREST of Mount Isarog, and elsewhere through much of the Philippines, lives a small fruit bat *(Haplonycteris fischeri)* that may hold the record for percentage of life spent pregnant. This little bat weighs only about 18 grams, and has a wingspan of about 30 centimeters. It flies at night beneath the forest canopy seeking out the ripe fruit of pepper plants, figs, wild bananas, and other forest plants. Like many bats, and many other rain-forest animals, dwarf fruit bats are long-lived, probably reaching 12 years of age. Small groups of closely-related females (mothers and daughters, aunts and nieces) live together with a single unrelated adult male, often roosting inside an old hollow tree or beneath a branch draped with moss. As is typical of long-lived animals, these little bats produce only a single young each year. For the first few weeks after they give birth, the mothers actually carry their babies with them when they forage for food. Remarkably, all of the females give birth each year within a period of a few days—not just all of the females in a group, but all of them inhabiting huge areas of the country. But they are not exceptional in that respect; other species of bats give birth in synchrony as well. What sets these bats apart is that the adult females all mate within two weeks of giving birth, and are pregnant for the rest of the year, every year. The females of this little bat are pregnant for 50 weeks each year, for their entire adult lives.

There are 25 species of fruit bats in the Philippines, most of which live for ten years or more and have very low rates of reproduction. Most live in social groups of related females.

ANT-PLANTS

PERHAPS THE MOST PECULIAR PLANTS in the Philippines are those that play host to ants: such flowering plants as *Myrmecodia*, *Hydnophytum*, *Hoya*, and *Dischidia*, and ferns including *Lecanopteris* and *Phymatodes*. The bases of the stems of *Hydnophytum* and *Myrmecodia* are greatly enlarged and honeycombed with tunnels through which an army of small ants transports food. The ants benefit from the shelter provided by the plant, while the plant gets part of its nutrition from the organic detritus left by the ants. The ants may also drive away other animals that would otherwise eat the plant.

Hoya and *Dischidia* are vines with milky sap belonging to the milkweed family. In some species of *Hoya*, the dome-shaped leaves grow very close to the bark of the tree trunks to which they cling. Each leaf extends many roots, holding the plant in place and absorbing moisture and nourishment from the nests of the ants that make their homes under the dome-leaves. On the other hand, some species of *Dischidia* produce two types of leaves: one small, the other greatly swollen and hollow. The latter collect water and provide homes for the ants. Roots extend from the stem into the hollow spaces in the leaves to absorb moisture and nutrients left by the ants.

Phymatodes and *Lecanopteris* are strange-looking ferns whose swollen, hollow rhizomes are inhabited by ants. *Phymatodes sinuosa* is a lowland species that grows only in the canopy, its thick, scaly rhizomes creeping along the branches of trees in moderately exposed places. At elevations higher than 1,000 meters, the strange *Lecanopteris carnosa* appears to be more common. Its rhizomes are green and pale blue-green when young, but turn black and horny with age. The young rhizomes form a thick crust around the branches of trees. Ants build nests in the safety of these elevated rhizomes. Small orchids and other plants often grow in the rhizome's crevices, germinating from seeds deposited by the ants and contributing to the development of tiny plant communities on tree branches high above the forest floor.

Plants of many different groups have evolved to attract ants to live with them, providing the ants with food and shelter. In return, the plants receive nutrients from the ants' droppings and protection from plant-eating animals.

COMMON ASIAN GHOST BAT

MOST KINDS OF BATS in the Philippines—48 species—feed on insects, although one does so with a twist. Insectivorous bats are almost certainly the most economically valuable mammals in the Philippines (as they are in most countries) because of the immense service they provide by consuming crop pests. A thousand bats in an attic—a fairly common occurrence—will almost certainly consume at least 50,000 insects every night; when these are the moths that feed on corn or rice, the savings to farmers can be substantial. Since colonies of bats in caves often number 10,000 to 100,000, and the caves in which they live number in the tens of thousands, it is evident that the beneficial impact can be huge. And, of course, if the bats are feeding on mosquitoes, we should be more grateful still.

Two general facts about bats are worth mentioning. First, the very negative attitude toward bats in the United States and Europe is not shared by most Asians, including many Filipinos, who view them as symbols of good luck. We know many people who not only tolerate but welcome bats in their houses. Second, and perhaps related to the first, the disease that is most feared in bats in the United States—rabies—has never been found in bats in the Philippines, despite repeated medical surveys. In the Philippines, rabies has been found almost exclusively in domestic dogs and cats.

The common Asian ghost bat (*Megaderma spasma*) is a little animal with a wingspan of only a foot or so. Nevertheless, it eats only the largest insects—cicadas, crickets, cockroaches, katydids, and large beetles and moths. The bats catch their prey not by using their sonar system (as most insectivorous bats do), but by listening with their huge ears for insects crawling noisily through the leaves or chirping to attract mates. Swooping down on the hapless, lovelorn insects, the bats put a permanent end to their reproductive efforts. There are frogs and lizards that make similarly inspired noises—and so, once in a while, the ghost bat catches and eats tiny frogs and lizards, the only bat in the Philippines—and one of only two in Asia—that does so.

The common Asian ghost bat (BOTTOM LEFT) is one of 48 species of insect-eating bats in the Philippines but is the only one that also eats frogs and lizards. Katydids (ABOVE), are among their usual prey. The yellow-faced horseshoe bat (BOTTOM RIGHT) is another member of this amazingly diverse group.

TREE FERNS

THE ANGLO-SAXON WORD *fearn,* meaning feather, gives us the English *fern*, alluding to the feather-like shape of this plant's leaves. In the Philippines, ferns are commonly called *paku*; a native speaker might wonder if there is a derivation from *pakpak*, meaning feather or wing. Unlike most plants, ferns do not produce flowers, fruits, or seeds. New ferns grow instead from microscopic spores found on the brown, dust-like clusters on the undersurfaces of mature leaves. Better suited than mosses for life on land, ferns have roots that conduct water and nutrients; with less danger of losing water to dry ground and air, some ferns grow so large they look like trees, with trunks two to seven meters high and up to one meter in diameter. These tree ferns, which are not real trees at all, do not develop wood. Their massive trunks are deceiving, actually consisting of interwoven roots surrounding a small middle stem less than ten centimeters in diameter.

In Southeast Asia, there are at least 190 species of tree ferns *(Cyathea)*, 37 of which are found in the Philippines. More than two-thirds of the Philippine species are unique to the country, and five of them are extremely rare and considered endangered: Their trunks are harvested for the local orchid-culture industry, either sawn as slabs or broken as potting mixtures for nurseries and greenhouses nationwide.

Distinctive and beautiful, tree ferns can grow to seven meters in height, and are present in most rain-forest habitats in the Philippines.

37

ELEPHANT-FOOT YAM

The solitary giant blossoms of the elephant-foot yam emit a stench like that of rotting meat, which is noticeable even from ten meters away.

EARLY EUROPEAN EXPLORERS returned from Southeast Asia with fantastic stories about a group of bizarre plants they had seen—elephant-foot yams. Over time, these stories became so exaggerated that they more resembled science fiction than hard science. The solitary giant blossoms of the elephant-foot yam emit a stench like that of rotting meat, which is noticeable even from ten meters away. The explorers claimed that the smell was so overpowering that anyone coming too close risked passing out. Nevertheless, we have studied them and have remained standing.

One species of these bizarre plants grows in the Philippines and is locally known as *pungapong (Amorphophallus campanulatus)*. It belongs to the jack-in-the-pulpit and skunk cabbage family. A perennial herb with a very large underground tuber 30 centimeters or more in diameter, the *pungapong* weighs about 25 kilograms. Its tuber sends out a single, very large leaf on a three-meter-high, purple-mottled stalk. A multicolored flower head later emerges with a thick, bell-shaped, ruffled cape (30 centimeters long, 45 centimeters across). Inside this giant flower head is a globular, cone-shaped flower stalk that is spongy, slightly wrinkled, and purple, and to which hundreds of minute flowers are attached. Male flowers are situated above female flowers, and beetles attracted by the smell of carrion transfer pollen from the males to the females. The flower stalk is warmer than the rest of the plant, a fact that is thought to be central in volatilizing and dispersing the odors.

After fertilization, in place of the female flowers, the stalk will bear numerous small fruits, green at first then turning yellow to red when ripe. Researchers have noticed that the stalk elongates slightly, presumably to display the ripe, juicy berries to birds that will eat them and disperse their seeds over great distances.

PHILIPPINE EAGLE

THE WILD ANIMAL BEST-KNOWN to most Filipinos, and the most widely recognized symbol for conservation, is the Philippine eagle *(Pithecophaga jefferyi),* the second-largest eagle in the world. These huge birds maintain populations only in old-growth lowland rain forest, although they will search for food in both old-growth and second-growth forest. They feed mostly on flying lemurs (also called kagwang), snakes, palm civets, flying squirrels, giant cloud rats, and occasional monkeys. From what little is known, adults choose mates with whom they remain throughout their very long lives (perhaps 20 years). They are remarkably inconspicuous, often sitting on perches at the heads of valleys while watching for prey, and only occasionally soaring long distances. Pairs live within territories of 20 to 50 square kilometers, usually constructing their nests in high treetops from which visibility is unusually good. They breed no more than once a year, and may skip years entirely; incubation of the single egg lasts about two months, and the young take about four months to reach the point of leaving the nest.

With such a low reproductive rate, and such a large home range, it is not surprising that the destruction of rain-forest habitat has been devastating to the Philippine eagle. Once found on most of the large islands of the country,

they are now believed to be extinct on all but Luzon and Mindanao, where the only large tracts of old-growth forest remain. Even worse, they can breed successfully only in lowland old-growth rain forest, the most ravaged habitat in the country. The total eagle population in 1996 was believed to be no more than 30 breeding pairs, most of which were confined to inaccessible mountains on Mindanao, and only a few of which inhabited the wilderness of the Sierra Madre Mountains of northern Luzon. Despite prolonged effort, attempts to breed them in captivity have been unproductive thus far. Protection of their forest habitat is clearly the only hope for their survival. The eagles' remaining habitats typically form critically important watersheds for coastal cities; since these areas are also excellent places for conservation of other species, their protection would have widespread benefits. As the nation's top carnivore and most dramatic and widely known species, the Philippine eagle's survival or extinction is watched as one of the most important indicators of environmental improvement or collapse.

RAFFLESIA

CONSIDER YOURSELF LUCKY INDEED if you have seen the giant flowers of *Rafflesia*. This strange plant lives as a parasite on the roots of vines related to the common grape. It produces neither leaves nor stems, only roots that penetrate and spread within the host plant. Rarely and unpredictably, the cabbage-like brown buds of *Rafflesia* emerge above ground, slowly opening to a flower like no other. One species on the Indonesian island of Sumatra *(Rafflesia arnoldii)* produces the largest flower on record, reaching up to a meter in diameter. *Rafflesia* can also claim the title of the stinkiest flower in the world: as with the elephant-foot yam (see page 38), the overpowering odor emitted by an opened flower can be mistaken for the smell of rotting meat. *Rafflesia*'s brownish-purple flower is unappealing to most insects, but carrion flies are attracted to the odor and color of these flowers and pollinate them. It will come as no surprise to learn that in the Malay language the plant is called *bunga-bangkay*—"the corpse flower."

This striking genus of strange parasites was named in honor of Sir Stamford Raffles, founder of Singapore. There are at least a dozen species in Southeast Asia, two of them unique to the Philippines. One is a small-flowered species, *Rafflesia manillana*, now listed as highly endangered. The other, large-flowered species, *Rafflesia schadenbergiana*, may be extinct. *R. manillana* has been seen in recent years on Mount Isarog, but *R. schadenbergiana* has not been seen since the first specimen was collected in 1882 on Mount Apo in southern Mindanao. Numerous attempts to find the species, most recently our own in 1994, have been unsuccessful. Deforestation by logging and agricultural clearing on the lower foothills of Mount Apo has apparently caused the extinction.

Rarely and

unpredictably,

the cabbage-

like brown buds

of Rafflesia

emerge above

ground, slowly

opening to a

flower like

no other.

The only part of a Rafflesia to appear above ground is the huge flower.

COLETO

MYNAS (and their close relatives the starlings) are widely known for their ability to mimic human speech, which emerges naturally from their own noisy communication and imitation of other species of birds. Most are colored black and gray, with occasional bands of white; many have yellow eyes, and some have yellow eye-rings that contrast sharply with their black feathers. A species found only in the Philippines, the coleto *(Sarcops calvus)*, takes this pattern to a striking extreme. Virtually the entire top of the coleto's head is bare skin of the brightest and most immodest pink, with not a feather to be seen. The sole exception is a narrow strip of black feathers that extends from the base of its bill over the top of its crown, the presence of which seems to emphasize the absence of feathers elsewhere. Its naked pink skin is entirely surrounded by the blackest of black feathers, and its eyes are almost equally dark, adding to the impact of the pink skin. On the back of its neck and upper shoulders is a mantle of silvery-white feathers; the rest of its body is a combination of contrasting gray and black. When the birds display, they erect this silvery-white mantle to form a shimmering background for the skin of the head—as if the contrasting black were not enough.

Unlike the great majority of birds (and other animals and plants) that are unique to the Philippines, coletos do not require old-growth forest; they seem to prefer shrubland and second-growth forest intermixed with mature rain forest. They do, however, require very tall dead trees in which to make holes and their nests; the nests are sometimes 35 meters above the ground. Because they so easily tolerate human disturbance, they are common and widespread, although heavily hunted to be kept as cagebirds.

Coletos are adaptable birds that live in both old-growth and disturbed forest.

Virtually the entire top of the coleto's head is bare skin of the brightest and most immodest pink, with not a feather to be seen.

41

LIZARDS

MOST PEOPLE GROWING UP in the Philippines grow up with lizards. Among the first wild animals seen by many children are the small house geckoes that emerge each evening. They cling upside down to the ceiling snapping up insects that are attracted to lights. Their barking calls are often the last sounds that children hear as they drift off to sleep.

These house geckoes are members of a family that includes at least 35 species in the Philippines, most of which live only in forest. Their amazing ability to hang upside down is due to lengthened fingers and expanded scales on both fore- and hind-feet; the scales are able to catch tiny projections from wood or painted surfaces, providing enough purchase to support their thin bodies. In a few species that live in forested areas, the enlarged feet have expanded even more, to the point that the lizards are able to use them as glider wings and sail from tree to tree. A group of lizards in a different family can spread their rib cages enormously to the sides, giving them the ability to "fly" as well.

There are altogether about 125 species of lizards in the Philippines, with about 99 unique to the country. In addition to the many kinds of geckoes and members of several less diverse groups, there are at least 65 species of skinks. The skinks are among the most active and conspicuous

animals on and near the ground in lowland forest during the daytime, noisily rustling through fallen leaves as they search for insects to eat. Several especially small skinks live beneath rocks; their legs are so tiny that they can barely be seen, and the lizards move by wriggling. (We have sometimes briefly mistaken them for earthworms.) Some other species live in cool, wet mossy forest; we have seen them only during the rather rare warm and sunny periods, basking on a branch before the fog rolls in.

Little is known in detail about the lives and ecology of most species of Philippine reptiles, and, as with frogs, a great many new species are currently being discovered—at least ten in the last five years. The limits of our information also make it difficult to know how many are endangered. We do know, though, that the majority of the more than 165 species of unique reptiles (including snakes, turtles, and lizards) require old-growth forest for their survival, and that many species are known to live only on one or a few islands. These two facts make it likely that a significant number of species are endangered by habitat destruction, but just how many remains for field biologists to determine.

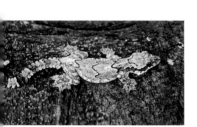

The huge feet of the "flying" gecko (TOP LEFT) **allow it to glide from tree to tree. Skinks are common forest lizards; some** (BOTTOM) **forage noisily through fallen leaves while others that have tiny legs** (TOP RIGHT) **move by wriggling sinuously, like a snake.**

WALING-WALING

WITH SOME 800 TO 1,000 SPECIES of orchids, the Philippines has one of the richest orchid floras in the world. By contrast, Canada and the United States, including Hawaii, Puerto Rico, and the Virgin Islands, have only 325 species among them. One might expect, then, to find orchids almost everywhere in the Philippine forest—as terrestrial orchids on the forest floor or above ground as epiphytes. Most are in fact epiphytic, which is aptly suggested by the Tagalog name *dapo sa kahoy* ("perched on tree limbs").

One of the most spectacular orchids, found only on Mindanao, is the waling-waling (*Euanthe sanderiana*). Dubbed the "queen of Philippine orchids," the waling-waling is so very distinct that botanists recently placed it in its own exclusive genus, *Euanthe*. The waling-waling is widely used in corsages and wedding bouquets, and is also popular among orchid breeders, who have produced many hybrids.

The waling-waling was first seen by botanists on Mindanao in 1882. Growing to a height of 60 to 120 centimeters, it starts to bloom when it is about 30 centimeters long and has a few sets of flat, channeled, and graceful recurved leaves. It has only one principal stem, only the terminal point of which is active. Flower clusters bear 12 to 16 flowers that open in succession, the blossoms usually lasting for about six weeks. The flower, the largest among Philippine orchids, is seven to twelve centimeters wide, and has a characteristic two-tone look. Closer inspection, however, reveals a change from pale purple blotched with dark reddish-purple at the top to lower sepals that are greenish with a pattern of netted lines and purple-crimson spots. The fruit ruptures at ripening, releasing thousands of minute seeds that can germinate only in the presence of a certain fungus.

Philippine orchids come in an amazing array of sizes, shapes, and colors. Most grow only in old-growth rain forest, often on branches of huge trees dozens of meters above the forest floor. Best known is the waling-waling (BOTTOM LEFT).

43

KAGWANG

Kagwang are nocturnal, gliding out from a tangle of vines and leaves or a hollow tree each evening as the sun sets.

THE COMMON NAMES of animals are sometimes descriptive and revealing—the purple-throated sunbird, for example, or even the rusty-crowned tree babbler. At other times, they are no help at all. A case in point is the animal sometimes called, in English, the Philippine flying lemur *(Cynocephalus volans)*, a species widespread on the southern islands that once were parts of the Ice-Age island of Greater Mindanao. These creatures are not lemurs, and they do not fly. They are, however, quite attractive, with beautiful dark eyes, a broad muzzle with a soft nose, soft wooly fur spotted with white, and an odd fold of skin between the front and hind limbs. The large fold of skin allows them to glide (not fly) between trees for distances up to 135 meters, much like North American and Asian flying squirrels.

Flying lemurs are, in all likelihood, related to bats, but they are so distantly related to bats or anything else that they and their one close relative (in Malaysia and Indonesia) are placed in their own Order by biologists. All monkeys, true lemurs, apes, and humans (253 species) make up one Order; all squirrels, beavers, rats, and their relatives (2,166 species) make up another, and so on; the two species of flying lemur have an Order all to themselves. Giving such unusual animals distinctive common names seems only right, and so we call them by their specific local names: kagwang in the Philippines and colugo in continental Asia.

Kagwang are nocturnal, gliding out from a tangle of vines and leaves or a hollow tree each evening as the sun sets. They eat only tender young leaves, but almost never more than a few from a single tree; they seem intent on sampling a little of everything in the forest. Unlike the great majority of unique Philippine mammals, kagwang actually prefer disturbed rain forest over old-growth, probably because many trees that grow in such places have sweeter leaves, without the tannins and alkaloid compounds that make old-growth plant leaves bitter. As a result, kagwang are more widespread, and their populations more stable, than many other Philippine mammals.

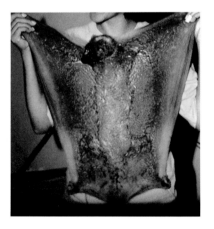

Distantly related to bats, the kagwang feeds on tender young leaves in the rain forest, gliding from tree to tree during the night and sleeping during the day. Babies ride along with their mothers for at least the first month of their lives.

SCREW PINES AND CLIMBING PANDANS

THE SCREW PINES *(Pandanus)*, so named for the peculiar spiral arrangement of their elongated, spiny leaves, grow on cliffs, sandy shores, and in beach forests. They can also grow in primary forests in the mountains up to 1,500 meters elevation. The Philippine species vary from small shrubs less than a meter tall to trees reaching 15 or more meters.

"Screw pine" also refers to the large, pineapple-like fruits of the more common and widely distributed species. Most of the Philippine species have prominent prop roots, structures that emanate from the trunk and reach to the ground like stilts, thus supporting the whole plant. There are nearly 50 species of screw pines in the Philippines, many of which are strictly localized.

One species, *Pandanus amaryllifolius*, has fragrant leaves that Filipinos use to flavor rice and other dishes. Since the leaves of screw pines are fibrous, resistant to decay, and grow very long, they are widely used in baskets, bags, hats, and mats. In the Bicol region, a species known to the Bicolanos as *karagomoi (Pandanus simplex)* is cultivated and used for basketry.

The climbing pandans *(Freycinetia)* are very conspicuous and attractive when in bloom. The male and female flowers, which grow on separate plants, are tightly packed in cylindrical structures called cones. The brilliant cones grow in clusters of three, surrounded by whorls of fleshy, reddish-orange bracts, then by long, slender, pointed leaves. The fragrant and fleshy bracts (specialized leaves supporting the flowers) are eaten only by the harpy fruit bat, *(Harpyionyteris whiteheadi)* whose whiskers and fur collect pollen from male flowers, which rubs off on the female flowers the animal visits later.

Plants of the screw pine family come in two forms, those that are erect and tree-like (THE GENUS *PANDANUS*; BOTTOM RIGHT), **and those that are vines** (THE GENUS *FREYCINETIA*; BOTTOM LEFT). **The flowers** (ABOVE LEFT) **and fruit of the viney pandans are eaten only by the harpy fruit bat, seen roosting above a patch of viney pandans** (BOTTOM LEFT). **The bats disperse the plants' pollen and seeds in the process.**

PITCHER PLANTS

PITCHER PLANTS *(Nepenthes)* are fantastic members of the diverse carnivorous-plant group that spurs so much popular curiosity, including ideas of man-eating plants (which remain mythological, so far as we know). The pitcher is actually part of a leaf, its upper portion modified early in its development to fold around itself, thus forming a pitcher complete with a lid. The pitcher collects rainwater into which the plant secretes digestive enzymes. Insects unfortunate enough to land near the slippery mouth fall into the liquid and are prevented from escaping by a series of downward-projecting spines. Eventually the insects drown and are digested by the plants.

There are 86 species of pitcher plants in the world, ten of which occur in the Philippines. Eight of the ten are unique to the country. The Philippines can boast of *Nepenthes merrilliana*, which has one of the largest pitchers, up to 34 centimeters deep, 14 centimeters wide, and holding as much as one and a half liters of liquid. The species is found only in Surigao on the island of Mindanao. Known as *lapsay* to the Manobo tribe that inhabits this region, the species flourishes in exposed or sunny edges of shrub lands from sea level up to 250 meters elevation. It grows in very poor, nutrient-deficient soil that is reddish in color and has very high iron content. We saw an abundance of pitcher plants at many of our study sites in the high mountains, festooning trees with their graceful, brightly colored pitchers.

Pitcher plants are vines with modified leaves that hold liquid containing enzymes. Insects that fall into the liquid eventually are digested by the plant.

PHILIPPINE FROGMOUTH

THE PHILIPPINE FROGMOUTH *(Batrachostomus septimus)* is perhaps the least typical bird in the Philippines, from its perpetually grumpy appearance to its way of making a living. But such idiosyncracy is a large part of what makes the overall diversity of birds possible.

Frogmouths are nocturnal, like owls, which probably accounts for their large eyes. They catch their prey by sitting on a limb and waiting until they see an insect moving on a branch or the ground, and then they pounce. Grasshoppers, cicadas, crickets, and beetles are snapped up eagerly into the large bill and capacious mouth. The nest, built on a horizontal branch two to five meters above the ground, is unusually simple but unique, made of downy feathers that the parents pluck from themselves and hold in place with a layer of spider webs, moss, and lichens. There they lay a single egg per season, which the male incubates during the day and the female at night.

These birds are probably common in lowland forest and maturing second growth, but because they are active at night, and apparently make no calls and sing no songs, they are inconspicuous and very poorly known. This species is unique to the Philippines, but may be found throughout the archipelago. A few related species are found from India to Australia.

A Philippine frogmouth protests its capture in a net. They are adaptable animals that live in both old-growth and disturbed forest, feeding on large insects such as cicadas and crickets.

The frogmouth's nest is made of downy feathers that the parents pluck from themselves and hold in place with a layer of spider webs, moss, and lichens.

VISAYAN SPOTTED DEER

With only a few hundred remaining in the wild, the Visayan spotted deer is one of the two most severely endangered species of deer in the world.

ONE OF THE MOST BEAUTIFUL MAMMALS in the Philippines is the Visayan spotted deer *(Cervus alfredi)*, a little animal that once lived on a set of islands in the central Philippines—Negros, Panay, Cebu, Masbate, and Guimaras, all of which were part of the Ice-Age island of Greater Negros-Panay. A healthy adult buck stands only 75 to 80 centimeters at the shoulder, not much larger than some dogs. Remarkably, this deer is closely related to the sambar deer of southern continental Asia, which can reach over a meter and a half at the shoulder, and weigh as much as 260 kilograms. This discrepancy in size illustrates one of the most consistent rules of island biogeography: Mammals that are large on mainland areas tend to be smaller on islands, and the larger they are on the mainland the more dramatically reduced they tend to be on the islands. In this light, the presence of a dwarf water buffalo on Mindoro seems less surprising (although one must still adjust to the sight of a buffalo less than a meter tall at the shoulder). Another surprising feature of this deer contributes to its beauty: It is one of the few species of deer that retains the spots it has as

a fawn throughout life. The result is a toy-like deer, the females so small that they appear to be babies, not the mothers of the even tinier deer standing near them.

Until the turn of the century, Visayan spotted deer were abundant, living from sea level to the mountaintops, preferring areas where fires, landslides, or other natural disturbances broke the forest canopy and brought tender plants close to the ground. Today, with only a few hundred remaining in the wild, they are one of the two most severely endangered species of deer in the world. Fortunately, a captive-breeding program begun a decade ago at Silliman University has successfully established a small but rapidly growing population that will be released into the wild when conditions in the countryside give them a fair chance of survival.

Visayan spotted deer were once found on all of the islands of Greater Negros-Panay, but are now down to a few hundred on Negros and Panay only. An adult buck (RIGHT) stands only about 75 centimeters at the shoulder.

PHILIPPINE PINES

MANY FILIPINOS SHARE fond memories of vacations in Baguio City, the "summer capital of the Philippines," where the cool climate and beautiful scenery bring relief from the oppressive heat in the lowlands. Baguio is in Benguet Province in the Central Cordillera, the mountain range that forms the backbone of northern Luzon. On these mountains, pine trees are the dominant vegetation. Easily recognized by their pyramidal shape, their needle-like leaves grouped in bunches of two or three, and their woody cones, two species of pine are native to the Philippines: the familiar Benguet pine or *saleng (Pinus insularis)* and the obscure Mindoro pine or *tapulao (Pinus merkusii)*.

The Benguet pine grows in the highlands of central and northern Luzon, and is dominant in Mountain Province from 1,000 to 2,500 meters elevation. During the Spanish colonial period, the pine's resin was an important commercial source of turpentine. The tree reaches a height of 40 meters and a diameter of 140 centimeters. The trunk is straight and the crown narrow, with short lateral branches.

The Mindoro pine is found in the Zambales peninsula of Luzon and in northwestern Mindoro. In its namesake region it occurs in pure stands even at low altitudes. The tree reaches a height of 25 meters and diameter of about 90 centimeters. The chief difference between the Mindoro and Benguet pines is that the needles of the former occur in groups of two while the needles of the latter develop in groups of three.

Both species are widely distributed from the Himalayas and Burma to the Philippines, suggesting that the Philippine populations were dispersed from mainland Asia.

There is considerable evidence that nearly the whole area now occupied by pines in the Philippines was formerly occupied by broad-leaved trees and shrubs. Yet a walk through the pine forest reveals that the ground is most often covered with grass while broad-leaved trees and shrubs are confined to moist ravines. The reason is that pines and grasses can withstand repeated fires, often man-made, that kill off broad-leaved trees and shrubs.

Two species of pines occur in mountainous regions of Luzon and Mindoro, prospering in areas where fires have killed other species of trees.

LEOPARD CAT

Large eyes, which help them to see as they forage at night, are set in a face delicately marked with fur of rich cinnamon-brown, cream, and black.

FOR MANY PEOPLE, "WILDLIFE" brings to mind images of elephants, lions, and bears. Large mammals are in fact relatively rare, accounting for only a few percent of all mammal species world-wide. There are even fewer animals of large size on islands, and among them predators are rarest of all. Island predators are usually small cats and raccoons or their equivalents, rather than lions and bears. These smaller carnivores may lack bulk, but make up for it in grace and beauty.

The Asian leopard cat *(Felis bengalensis)* is one such species, and is the only true cat in the Philippines (there are also two species of palm civets that are sometimes called civet-cats). They are small and delicate, and those that are found in the Philippines do not often exceed the size of a big house cat. Large eyes, which help them to see as they forage at night, are set in a face delicately marked with fur of rich cinnamon-brown, cream, and black. The leopard cat occurs widely in Asia and so is not unique to the Philippines, but the two local populations (on Palawan and on Greater Negros-Panay) have recently been named as distinct subspecies.

These little cats once lived from sea level up to at least the lower levels of montane forest at 1,500 meters. Although they can climb a bit, they are not arboreal, so they naturally prefer places where fires, landslides, or floods create openings for the brush in which their prey live at ground level. They feed on rodents, small birds, and large insects; the cats are far too small to kill even a baby pig or deer.

When humans began to cut down the forest, the cats probably prospered at first, since much of the land was left to regrow into just the kind of habitat the cats like. They are adaptable enough to survive even in forested gulleys adjacent to sugar-cane fields, where they once performed a great service by catching and killing rats that ate the crops. Unfortunately, the cats also occasionally preyed on the chickens that plantation workers raise. Since the workers can sell leopard-cat kittens as pets and the pelts of adults as curiosities, the cats have suffered badly. The overall result of hunting and habitat destruction is that the cats are now uncommon on Palawan, quite rare on Negros and Panay, and probably extinct on Cebu.

Leopard cats feed on small rodents and birds in a wide range of habitats on the Ice-Age islands of Greater Palawan and Greater Negros-Panay. They are now rare in the few places where they survive.

KAPA-KAPA

ONE OF THE MOST SPECTACULAR flowering epiphytes (see page 32) is the kapa-kapa *(Medinilla magnifica)*. Growing on the limbs of trees in the lowland rain forests of Luzon and Mindoro, it is one of the 80 species of *Medinilla* found in the Philippines. Its squarish, corky stems sprout relatively large, glossy, elliptical leaves that are rich emerald in color. The species name, *magnifica*, evokes the plant's magnificent blossoms, an explosion of pink to coral-red flowers.

Kapa-kapa has been cultivated since the middle of the 19th century, when it was first collected and formally described, by the English collector J. H. Veitch. In 1854, the Royal Horticultural Society of England bestowed its grand prize on the plant. Then and now regarded as one of the most gorgeous and striking tropical plants in cultivation, its growing fame encouraged garden enthusiasts to seek out and gather more plants from the wild. Veitch tried to frus-trate their efforts and keep his trade secret by reporting that he had found the plant on the island of Java in Indonesia. We know now that his report was erroneous; the kapa-kapa is unique to the Philippines.

The species is becoming exceedingly rare in its native habitat because of forest destruction, which opens up the canopy. The kapa-kapa prefers cool, shaded areas, and deforestation deprives it of this optimum environment. There are in all likelihood more kapa-kapa specimens growing in cultivation than living in the wild.

A spectacular and popular cultivated plant, the kapa-kapa is now quite rare in the wild because of destruction of lowland rain forest.

The kapa-kapa prefers cool, shaded areas, and deforesta-tion deprives it of this optimum environment.

FLAME-TEMPLED BABBLER

Nineteen species of babblers are found in the Philippines, 18 of them occurring nowhere else. Ten of these beautiful, unique species are seriously threatened by destruction of their rain-forest habitat.

AMONG OUR FAVORITE BIRDS on nearly every mountain where we have worked are the babblers, a family that includes 19 species in the Philippines. These little birds make cheerful, melodious calls through much of the day as they forage in flocks for small insects, fruits, and berries. Their short, rounded wings flap so rapidly they produce a soft buzzing sound. They do not seem to be afraid of people, often surrounding us in singing, buzzing, brightly colored flocks. We have seen several of the babblers that live at high elevations drinking from the water-filled cups of pitcher plants.

One of the prettiest of these species is the flame-templed babbler *(Stachyris speciosa)* of Negros and Panay. Bright yellow patches of feathers at the base of its beak, on its neck, and the front of its crown contrast with black and iridescent green on the rest of its head and neck. During courtship, the species prominently displays a tuft of long, orange-yellow feathers that is just behind each eye. For some babblers, courtship includes elaborate food-begging displays in which adults imitate the begging behavior of their babies.

Eighteen of the 19 species of babblers in the Philippines are unique; only one species that lives on Palawan can be found elsewhere, on Borneo. Because their short wings make them poorly suited for long-distance flying, it is not surprising that most of the species live on only one of the Ice-Age islands. Ten of the babblers are listed as endangered (several quite seriously endangered) because of destruction of their rain-forest habitat. Nearly all of the forests in which they live are watershed areas for cities and agricultural lands.

ALMACIGA

WHAT THE REDWOOD is to California, the giant almaciga (*Agathis philippensis*) is to the Philippines. The almaciga, one of the few species of conifers that can grow in the humid tropics, is a relative of the New Zealand kauri pine (*Agathis australis*). Both almaciga and kauri belong to a family of evergreens found only in the Southern Hemisphere whose ancestors first appeared in the Jurassic Period, about 150 million years ago. Fossil records indicate that members of the genus *Agathis* made their way from the Australian region into Southeast Asia during the Ice Age when sea levels were lower and the channels between islands were narrower.

Almaciga is a huge tree, up to 60 meters tall and with a trunk three meters wide. Its bark is grayish brown and forms large, flat, angular scales resembling jigsaw-puzzle pieces. Its massive trunk is cylindrical, straight, and clear of branches until it reaches the narrowly conical crown where it radiates into slender whorls of stiffly projecting branches. Both male and female cones are produced on these branches; the female cones are much larger than the male cones, taking two years to mature. Seeds may be fertilized with pollen from either the same tree or from another nearby. The seeds have wings that allow them to float away from the parent tree when the cone breaks into pieces.

Almaciga yields a valuable resin known in the world market as Manila copal and used in the manufacture of varnishes and linoleum. Tapping the resin has been an important source of income for many rural people in the Philippines. Almaciga is now listed as a potentially threatened species because excessive tapping coupled with destructive methods (such as application of sulfuric acid to stimulate resin production) has killed many trees. With other sources of hardwood timber diminishing, the industry is turning its eyes on almaciga, which is highly prized and carries a premium on the market. We can only hope that the almaciga does not meet the fate of the kauri pine, which was exploited to exhaustion in New Zealand during the first half of this century.

Beads of resin at the base of the trunk of an almaciga; this resin is used to make a fine varnish. Over-tapping and logging have greatly reduced the number of almaciga, the largest tree in the Philippines.

With other sources of hardwood timber diminishing, the industry is turning its eyes on almaciga, which is highly prized and carries a premium on the market.

PHILIPPINE TUBE-NOSED FRUIT BAT

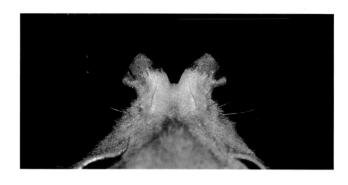

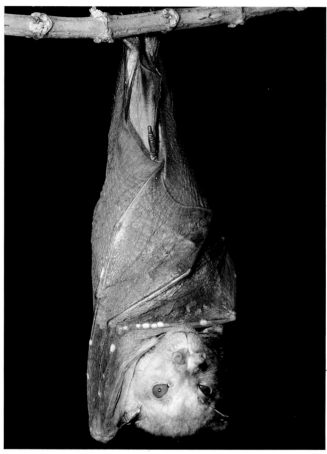

Probably now reduced to about one percent of its original population size, the Philippine tube-nosed fruit bat survives only in narrow bands of lowland forest on two or three islands. The photo at left, taken from above the bat's head, shows the peculiar development of the nostrils.

THERE ARE AT LEAST 73 species of bats in the Philippines, of which 25 are fruit bats. Among the strangest bats—admittedly an odd lot, even to someone who likes them—is a species discovered in 1984 and now documented on three islands in the center of the country. The tube-nosed fruit bat *(Nyctimene rabori)* is average-sized by Philippine standards, with a wingspan of about 55 centimeters (22 inches or so). But many things about its appearance are not at all usual. Among other oddities, it is one of the few striped bats in the world—in this case, one broad dark stripe down the center of its back. Even so, most people would not immediately notice the stripe, but would focus instead on either the odd yellow spots dotting its ears and wings or, more likely, the bizarre nostrils that resemble scrolls of soft leather projecting above its mouth. Its fur is soft, generally the color of honey, and its eyes are large, dark, and gentle.

Tube-nosed fruit bats live in the remaining lowland rain forests of Negros, Cebu, and Sibuyan, at elevations up to about 1,250 meters. They roost in the forest, probably either in vegetation or large hollow trees, but never in caves; the limited evidence suggests that they rarely fly far from home and virtually never venture out into agricultural land. Like so many other fruit bats, they feed mostly on wild figs, and seem to be partial to soft, over-ripe fruit.

Lowland rain forest on Cebu is virtually gone; if these bats still survive there (they were seen only once, ten years ago), they do so tenuously. On Sibuyan, only a small population survives in the hills. The largest population lives on Negros Island, where less than one percent of their old-growth lowland forest habitat remains. These bats, and the other species dependent on lowland forest, now live principally, perhaps entirely, in narrow ribbons of forest, usually only a few hundred meters wide, around the shoulders of two mountains in the southern part of the island and two in the north. Each year, illegal logging and clearing reduce the limited forest habitat still further; each dry season, more of the rain forest goes up in smoke.

RATTANS

ALMOST SYNONYMOUS WITH fine articles of world-famous Philippine handicrafts, such as furniture, baskets, cords, and walking sticks, rattans *(Calamus)* are climbing members of the palm family. Creeping and twisting along the forest floor and climbing tall trees to reach sunlight in the canopy, rattans can reach a length of 150 meters. Rattan cane comes from pieces of the jointed stem, the distance between joints reaching more than a meter. Unlike bamboo, rattan is solid inside, and unlike wood, its fibers run the length of the plant in a single direction. These characteristics give rattan remarkable strength and flexibility.

The young parts of these climbing palms are usually armed with numerous stiff, needle-sharp spines. The leaf stalks are also spiny, as are other parts of the plant, which may have stout and sharp claws. Most of us who have ventured into the forest have unpleasant memories of being snagged by the spines of the stems. The long, whip-like extensions of the leaves can lift off your hat or grasp your shirt. Once entangled, only discretion and patience will rid you of these exasperating snares.

Harvesting rattan in the wild demands great courage and skill. Because of over-harvesting in more accessible locations, rattan is currently sought in very steep and treacherous areas, including 100-meter sheer cliffs. In 1987, a harvester was killed in a fall from one such cliff near our field camp on Leyte.

Most of the 80-plus species of rattans in the Philippines are endemic. One, *Calamus merrillii*, locally called *palasan*, is officially listed as threatened due to excessive harvesting. In the past, rattans were classified as minor forest products, but today they are an increasingly valuable commodity. The incentive to collect them as a supplementary source of income for people living near the forest will certainly put pressure on the remaining populations. In the Philippines, rattan is not cultivated, but only extracted from the wild.

Most of us who have ventured into the forest have unpleasant memories of being snagged by the spines. Once entangled, only discretion and patience will rid you of these exasperating snares.

TAMARAW

One of the most distinctive and seriously endangered mammals in the world, the tamaraw of Mindoro Island probably numbers fewer than two hundred individuals due to habitat destruction, over-hunting, and mismanagement.

IN THE NINETEENTH CENTURY, the island of Mindoro, heavily forested and long avoided because of an especially virulent strain of malaria, was called "the dark island" by many outsiders. Although it is not far from Manila, it was poorly known in many respects, especially its fauna and flora. In 1888, the scientific community was startled by the announcement of the discovery on Mindoro of the largest mammal native to the Philippines—the dwarf water buffalo, now better known as the tamaraw *(Bubalus mindorensis)*. The local people, who had hunted them with spears and snares for centuries, feared them because of their inclination to turn and gore their attackers. Barrel-chested and only a little over a meter tall at the shoulder, these buffalo weigh roughly 200 kilograms—about 450 pounds of tough muscle, bone, and sinew. At one time they lived throughout most of the island, from forest at sea level to the mountaintops at 2,000 meters; there may have been as many as 10,000 of them at the turn of the century. They preferred places where there had been fires or landslides that promoted the growth of grass or other vegetation near the ground. Their small size and great strength enabled them to push through dense jungle and climb steep mountains.

With the advent of anti-malarial medicines near the turn of the century, Mindoro became safer and more accessible. Loggers cut the prime trees from lowland rain forest, plantation owners brought in laborers and their families to clear the lowlands for sugar cane and other crops, and subsistence farmers from Luzon and other densely populated places moved to Mindoro in search of farmland. The local people, many of whom had traditionally kept small herds of cattle, burned the degraded forest to encourage the spread of the grass on which their cattle fed.

As word of the tamaraw and its reported ferocity spread, hunters eager to prove their bravery shot the animals in increasing numbers (the traditional spears were not favored by those who had guns—the odds shifted too much in favor of the tamaraw). A shipment of cattle in the 1930s brought rinderpest (an acutely infectious disease that causes inflammation of the intestines) that spread to the tamaraw and decimated its population. By the late 1940s, tamaraw numbers had plummeted to about 1,000, and fell to roughly 175 by 1983. Several reserves were established beginning in 1936, but none was given much actual protection. The swelling population of landless plantation laborers, the indigenous people, and hunters from Manila and outside the country continued to prey on the tamaraw. Hunters with automatic weapons arrived from Manila in helicopters during the 1960s and 1970s, and reportedly in the early 1980s as well. A captive-breeding program, one of the best-funded wildlife programs in the country during the 1960s to 1980s, succeeded in capturing many wild animals. The project was ended in the early 1990s when it became apparent that nearly all of the animals had died soon after capture, and that little of the funding had reached the project site. No reliable estimate of the tamaraw population currently exists, but there is no reason to believe that the number has increased since the 175 counted in 1983. Controversy pervades discussions about what actions should be taken, with the result that little is being done.

WRITHED-BILLED HORNBILL

RAUCOUS, BIG, AND BRASSY, hornbills once inhabited all of the larger islands of the Philippines and figure prominently in the folklore of many parts of the country. Each of the five species exhibits geographic variation, with each of the Ice-Age islands having its own uniquely colored population. Some taxonomists now argue that each of these is a distinct species. The complexity of this issue underscores the fact that hornbills, like most other Philippine animals, still show the effects of the distant past when sea levels were lower and broad land-bridges connected many of the islands.

The bills of these birds are enormous and usually brightly colored. The top of the bill is a hollow structure called a casque that serves as a resonating chamber for the bird's calls. Hornbills eat a wide range of foods (including mice and nestling birds), but depend primarily on wild figs in old-growth lowland rain forest, as do many other birds, mammals, and insects. They forage high in the canopy in small flocks that are almost always family groups, noisily calling to each other as they spot interesting things to eat or potential predators; they are said to take special pleasure in pestering the larger but less maneuverable Philippine eagles. Like most large birds, they reproduce very slowly and live for a long time (perhaps as long as 20 years), and take great care raising their young. When the female is ready to lay eggs, the male brings mud that the pair fashions into a solid wall covering most of the opening into their tree-hole nest. The female stays inside the tree-hole to incubate the eggs and nestlings until the young are ready to fly, entirely dependent on her mate to bring food for herself and their brood.

Animals that reproduce as slowly as writhed-billed hornbills *(Aceros waldeni)* are generally unable to sustain heavy hunting pressure, and those that require lowland rain forest are especially vulnerable to drastic population decline when the forest is logged. This double jeopardy has hit the hornbills hard: Each day, the harsh but familiar and distinctive calls of hornbills echo through fewer and fewer valleys in the Philippines. Many local populations are extinct, and many of those remaining are critically endangered. The writhed-billed hornbill and several of the species/subspecies from the Ice-Age island of Greater Negros-Panay are virtually extinct, and a distinctive population from Ticao Island is believed to be the first hornbill in the world to have become extinct.

A young tarictic hornbill from Negros Island.

Hornbills are among the most conspicuous and distinctive birds in the Philippines. Writhed-billed (LEFT; FEMALE AND MALE) **Visayan tarictic** (TOP RIGHT; FEMALE AND MALE) **and Sulu** (BOTTOM RIGHT; MALE) **hornbills are critically endangered in most of the areas where they survive.**

APITONG AND OTHER DIPTEROCARPS

MANY GIANT TREES of the lowland rain forest are members of the hardwood family called dipterocarps, known to Filipinos by such names as *apitong*, *bagtikan*, *lauan*, *tangile*, *guijo*, and *yakal*. The crowns of these trees extend 30 to 50 meters high, and their trunks may reach almost two meters in diameter. Reinforced with buttresses that flare out from the base of the tree, the trunk grows straight and is 25 to 30 meters long, characteristics that make these trees especially desirable as timber. Dipterocarps once constituted 80 percent of the country's timber resources and provided the bulk of what is sold on the world market as "Philippine mahogany." Although best used for fine furniture, these woods have also been used for railroad ties, utility poles, bridges and wharfs, pulp, paper, and plywood. One species *(Dipterocarpus grandiflorus)*, known as *apitong* in the Tagalog language and *agagkag* in Visayan, yields an oily resin, called *balaw*, which is used in lamp oil, varnish, and caulking compounds.

Forty-five species of dipterocarps are indigenous to the Philippines, of which nearly half are found nowhere else. The current distribution of these trees in the Philippines resulted from the configuration of land during the last glacial period, with many dipterocarp species confined to a single Ice-Age island. Even though the fruits of dipterocarps have wing-like appendages that produce a parachute-like motion when they fall, they are too heavy to be carried far from the parent tree; many land directly under the tree, leading to overcrowding and forcing them to compete for space. The seeds cannot survive long periods at sea. These limitations on the dispersal of the seeds isolated populations and led to the evolution of many new species.

Philippine old-growth dipterocarp forests have almost entirely disappeared. Several species once fairly common in primary lowland forests in many parts of the country have been decimated by logging and slash-and-burn agriculture. These trees generally take at least 40 years to produce their first seeds, and 100 years to reach timber size. Ever-increasing demand and the nearly exhausted supply have made logging companies even more zealous to exploit the last remnants of forests on Palawan, Mindanao, and Luzon.

Once the primary base for the logging industry in the Philippines, apitong and other dipterocarps have been so heavily over-exploited that the nation has begun importing timber.

PHILIPPINE CROCODILE

ALTHOUGH FEARED IN NEARLY every place they live, crocodiles—including the freshwater species *Crocodylus mindorensis* that is unique to the Philippines—are among the best of parents. After a long and often noisy courtship, the female Philippine crocodile builds a large, deep nest of layered soil and vegetation, which is heated by decomposing plants. She then lays as many as 40 eggs, which she tends carefully for about 18 hours daily for the next three months, adding, removing, and shifting soil and vegetation to maintain just the right temperature for her offspring. As hatching time approaches, she becomes increasingly aggressive, chasing away other crocodiles and any potential predators. When the young emerge from their eggshells, their chirping calls alert the mother, who carefully digs into the nest to release them from the layers of soil and vegetation overhead.

Philippine crocodiles are a dwarf species, usually less than two meters in length, although rare individuals may reach nearly three meters. They live in freshwater lakes, rivers, and marshes, where they feed on fish, waterbirds, lizards, and snakes. Babies prey on insects, small fish, and frogs. In contrast, the estuarine crocodiles that live in brackish and salt water in the Philippines and elsewhere from Asia to Australia typically reach four to five meters in length and feed on large fish and turtles.

Both species have been severely over-hunted in the Philippines. Their populations are additionally threatened by toxic wastes from mines, destruction of marshes and riverine habitats, and the conversion of lakes for fishponds. Wild Philippine crocodiles, which once numbered well over 10,000, were reduced to fewer than 1,000 by 1982. At last count in 1993, there were only about 100 individuals left in the wild. Although they were once widespread throughout the Philippines, the only viable wild populations today are in Mindanao and possibly Mindoro.

Hunting appears to be continuing unabated, even though the crocodiles are now protected under the law; the Philippine crocodile is listed as one of the most severely endangered crocodiles in the world. Current captive-breeding programs have excellent funding and facilities and have had some success, but as with other endangered species, protection of the crocodiles' natural habitats seems the best course in the long run, since these lakes, rivers, and marshes are of critical importance to the stability of watersheds and marine fisheries.

Philippine crocodiles, which once numbered well over 10,000, were reduced to fewer than 1,000 by 1982. At last count in 1993, there were only about 100 individuals left in the wild.

PHILIPPINE BARE-BACKED FRUIT BAT

Workers from a nearby sugar-cane plantation dig guano during times when there is no field work. Smoke from their fires, destruction of lowland rain forest, and hunting by plantation workers led to the extinction of the Philippine bare-backed fruit bat by the early 1980s. The only existing photographs are of museum specimens stuffed with cotton (ABOVE).

IN THE LOWLAND FOREST of Negros Island once lived another fruit bat, a bit larger than the tube-nosed bat and belonging to a group called bare-backed bats *(Dobsonia chapmani)*—so named because the leathery part of their wings attached to the body up near their spine, giving the appearance that they had no fur on their backs (though it was actually present beneath the skin of the wings). These bats roosted in caves near the coast, in rooms near the mouths where dim light penetrated. The roosting colonies would swell when adult females came together to give birth to their single young during April and May, near the end of the dry season. Each evening, the bats would fly out to feed on fruit in both old-growth and lightly disturbed lowland rain forest.

At the end of World War II, 60 percent of Negros was still covered by rain forest. As subsidies for sugar increased, virtually all of the flat lowlands were cleared for plantations. Subsistence farmers who had occupied some of this land were forced higher into the hills, clearing the upper reaches of lowland forest. When work in the cane fields was not available, plantation workers, paid barely enough to survive, would mine guano (bat excrement) from caves and sell it as fertilizer for a few pesos. They lit the caves with small fires, whose smoke accumulated in asphyxiating clouds in the cave ceilings. Bats of many species that fell from the ceilings were roasted over the fires, a welcome source of protein to the impoverished workers.

By the mid-1980s, the last of the forest on Negros below 800 meters elevation had been cleared, and the remnants of upland forest covered only six percent of the island. With the ascendancy of sugar-cane plantations, the rural poor remained as impoverished as ever, but the guano, and the bats that produced it, were nearly gone. The largest of the bats, those that lived near the entrances to the caves and offered the most meat, had disappeared entirely—the first mammalian species in the Philippines to be documented as extinct in modern times.

The nation now faces stark alternatives: a decline from the biologically richest place on earth to environmental devastation, or recovery from the current brush with disaster to a point of stability.

The Causes and Effects of Deforestation

LAWRENCE R. HEANEY

WHEN THE FIRST HUMANS ARRIVED in the Philippines from adjacent Asia many thousands of years ago, they found an archipelago that was remarkably rich in natural resources. The seas were inhabited by the earth's most diverse marine communities, providing an abundant source of food throughout the year. The land was covered almost entirely by rain forest that provided them with building materials, meat from wildlife, and seemingly everlasting supplies of clear, cool water.

Those natural resources have been squandered, so badly damaged by over-use, mismanagement, and greed that recovery is uncertain, and collapse seems to be a real possibility. The nation now faces stark alternatives: a decline from the biologically richest place on earth to environmental devastation, or recovery from the current brush with disaster to a point of stability. To understand the origin of this dramatic and terrible situation, we must begin with history, but must end with societal and personal choice.

THE LOST FOREST

Few countries in the world were originally more thoroughly covered by rain forest than the Philippines. Brazil has extensive savannah and brush; Indonesia has many dry islands; Kenya and Tanzania have only small patches of rain forest. A few hundred years ago, at least 95 percent of the Philippines was covered by rain forest; only a few patches of open woodland and seasonal forest, mostly on Luzon, broke the expanse of moist, verdant land.

By the time the Spanish arrived in the Philippines in the 16th century, scattered coastal areas had been cleared

The moist tropical climate resulted in luxuriant rain forest that once covered at least 95 percent of the Philippines, harboring one of the highest densities of unique species anywhere on earth. Lake Balinsasayao (ABOVE) is one of the most beautiful places on Negros Island.

for agriculture and villages. The only domestic grazer was the water buffalo, and pastureland was very limited. Some forest had been cleared in the interior as well—particularly the terraced rice lands of the Central Cordillera of northern Luzon—but most coastal areas and the richest of the lowlands remained completely forested, broken only by the occasional cultivated clearings. By 1600, the human population of the Philippines probably numbered about 500,000, and old-growth rain forest covered 90 percent of the land, home to thousands of plant and animal species interacting in the web of life that sustained the human population.

At the end of more than 300 years of Spanish colonial rule, rain forest still covered about 70 percent of the Philippines. Some islands had been heavily deforested, while others remained nearly untouched. Cebu was so badly deforested that ornithologists visiting the island in the 1890s reported that they could find no old-growth forest at all, and the neighboring islands of Bohol and Panay had less than half of their original forest. Although the fertile lowland plains of Luzon had largely been cleared by this time, much of the highland rain forest remained intact. Mindoro's rain forest was protected by an especially virulent strain of malaria, Palawan's by its isolation, and Mindanao's was largely left untouched because of the aggressive independence of the Moro people. The plant and animal communities retained their integrity, readily able to provide resources to human populations in all but a few places.

In 1992, the date of the most recent forest survey, old-growth rain forest had declined to a shocking 8.6 percent. By late 1997, that percentage has probably dropped to seven percent, and perhaps further still. The extent of rain-forest

OLD-GROWTH FOREST COVER, 1900 AND 1992

Old-growth rain forest covered about 70 percent of the Philippines in 1900. By 1992, that had been reduced to only about eight percent, in scattered, usually small, fragments.

forest in 1900

forest in 1992

Redrawn from National Mapping and Resource Information Authority, 1988.

destruction in the Philippines may represent another "first": In addition to probably having the highest density of both unique and endangered species in the world, its decline in old-growth forest from 70 percent to seven percent in less than a century is probably the most rapid and severe in the world. This destruction is the primary reason the Philippines is ranked as having the most severely endangered mammal and bird faunas in the world. The degradation is also responsible for the increasing floods and droughts in the country, as well as massive erosion, coral-reef siltation, and ground-water depletion.

NEGROS ISLAND: A CASE STUDY IN DEFORESTATION

Destruction of rain forest is not inevitable, and it is not a requirement of "progress." In the long run, it is seldom defensible in economic or social terms, since it usually represents a net loss for the great majority of the people who live in the area. It is also a great loss for the plants and animals affected. And yet it has happened rapidly in the Philippines, bringing challenges that we did not anticipate and for which we are poorly prepared.

The magnitude of these social, economic, and environmental issues is daunting; a comprehensive understanding of the process of forest destruction as it has unfolded for the entire nation would require more time, space, and knowledge than we have available in this book. Taking a single

In many places in the Philippines, such as this area in western Leyte, the narrow coastal plain is backed by steep mountain slopes.

island as an example seems the best way to bring the issues surrounding deforestation to a manageable scale. We have chosen Negros Island, near the center of the Philippines, as our case study, not because it is exceptional, but rather because in most respects it is quite ordinary—an ordinary example of biotic and environmental devastation.

When the Spanish conducted the first census of Negros Island in the early 1600s, the population was about 25,000, as it probably had been for centuries. Most of the inhabitants lived in small villages along the coast, especially near the mouths of the few small rivers. Hunters often hiked the short distance to the mountains (less than a one-day journey) to set snares for wild pig and deer, and fisherfolk slashed and burned small clearings in order to grow vegetables and medicinal plants for a few years. With the rain-catching mountains rising to about 2,000 meters in both the north and the south, rivers from the peaks always carried water, even when the dry season stretched to three or four months.

For the next two hundred years, little changed on Negros Island. In the early 1800s, censuses showed at most 30,000 people, and only a little more land had been cleared along the fertile west coast. But by 1850, external factors began to change conditions dramatically.

The first of these factors was the arrival of modern medicine, specifically the smallpox vaccine. Brought across the Pacific Ocean from Mexico as live culture in orphaned boys, the vaccine had an immediate impact. Previously, smallpox had swept through the villages on Negros every three to five years, often killing a quarter or more of the young children. With the vaccine, mortality dropped dramatically, causing the first upswing in population growth in centuries. Other medicines arrived soon after, allowing more people to live to the age at which they, too, could produce families.

A second factor with even greater and more far-reaching impact was the arrival of large-scale, export-based plantation agriculture, especially sugar cane. Tobacco, manila hemp, and cotton had been cultivated on huge haciendas elsewhere in the Philippines since the 1700s, but it was only with the boom in sugar prices in the 1850s that wealthy landowners from Panay began developing similar operations on Negros. The fertile western plains were quickly cleared of prime lowland rain forest, as were smaller areas on the east coast. Workers from Negros joined immigrants from the more densely populated neighboring islands of Panay and Cebu in the swelling ranks of those planting and cutting cane.

Until the development of petroleum-powered machinery, export-based plantation agriculture depended entirely on the supply of human hand-labor. Then as now, the price of a given product—sugar in this case—was determined globally based on competition between producers to sell for the lowest price (except in the case of subsidies, which are discussed below). Various mechanisms were developed in different parts of the world to assure a ready supply of the material most critical to competitiveness on the world market— cheap human labor. In the Western Hemisphere, the mechanism was often slavery, mostly involving transplanted Africans; in Europe, it was serfdom, peasantry, or something similar. The Spanish in the Philippines developed a system that was similar to serfdom, although without the formality of a titled landed gentry.

In this system, the colonial government sold, or gave as a reward for service, large tracts of land to certain individuals. The people whose families had lived in the area for generations were required to provide labor for a brief portion of each year as a form of taxation. Initially this system operated on a small scale, but as the export market grew, little good land remained for small farmers, and so more local people chose to work in the fields for wages. With the advent of large-scale sugar-cane production on Negros Island, great numbers of workers were brought from other islands specifically to work the fields; they helped to keep the price of labor low, and were especially dependent on the landowners for their survival. The combination of low wages and high prices for food and clothing locked workers into a cycle of dependency exacerbated by their need for cash loans from the landowners during the the seasons when there was no work.

Educational opportunities for plantation workers were minimal, and in a society made up only of wealthy landowners, a small merchant class, and a large population of people who worked in the fields and kept small subsistence farms in the nearby hills, there were almost no opportunities for other employment. Virtually the only way a family

POPULATION DENSITY AND FOREST COVER

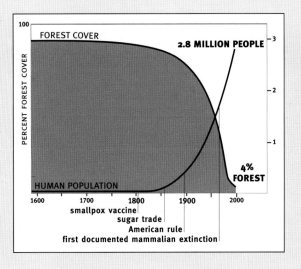

Once plantations began to develop on Negros Island in the 1850s, logging operations and the surging population of impoverished farmers and plantation workers led to the near-complete destruction of the rain forest that once covered almost the entire island. Only scattered fragments remain in the most rugged, mountainous areas.

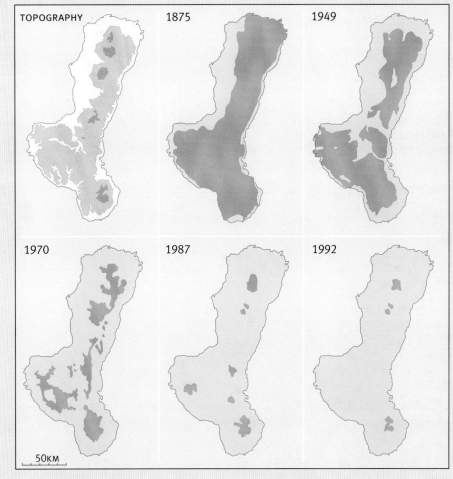

Commercial logging has led the way in destruction of rain forest since the 1800s, but surged dramatically in the 1960s and 1970s. Fees and taxes paid by logging companies have generally been extremely low. This photo was taken on Mount Busa, Mindanao, in 1993.

could increase its income was to produce more children to work on the plantations. Futhermore, the only security in old age lay in those same children; indeed, the only valuable "possession" of such people was their family. And so people produced large families in an attempt to secure their individual futures, but in the process they guaranteed a supply of the most valued commodity in a plantation-based society—abundant, cheap human labor. By the late 1800s, the population on Negros Island had climbed from 25,000 to about 500,000 people.

The third influential factor contributing to swift and massive change in the lives of people on Negros was the installation of the American colonial government in 1898. After fighting one of the bloodiest wars in its history in suppressing the independence movement and taking control of the Philippines, the United States colonial government built new schools and clinics and increased the amount of business activity, thereby creating new sources of employment. It also granted concessions to logging companies, encouraging them to cut new roads into the interior forests of Negros and other islands, opening the land to logging and then to a steady stream of workers leaving the plantations to find farmland of their own. Plantation agri-

culture was further expanded and intensified as the colonial government sought ways to generate foreign currency from exported raw materials and unprocessed foodstuffs. Lumber companies operating on Negros cut the remaining prime lowland forest before moving on to other islands to do the same. The result was swelling population and reduced forest cover.

From 500,000 in 1898, the population of Negros climbed to nearly 2,000,000 in 1970 and to about 3,000,000 today, at a density of 220 per square kilometer, which is twice that of France and nearly eight times that of the United States. Old-growth forest cover declined from 90 percent in the 1700s to about 60 percent at the end of World War II. The continued expansion of sugar-cane fields onto hillsides during the 1950s and 1960s was made possible by United States government subsidies to the sugar industry. These subsidies were initially intended to stimulate an economy weakened by World War II, and later to prop up a friendly government during the U.S. war in Vietnam. Unfortunately, an unintended side-effect of the subsidies was to encourage the plantation owners to maintain their old, inefficient hand-labor system. The subsidies also made it economically feasible for them to clear and farm steep, easily eroded hillsides and turn a tidy profit; without the subsidies, these hillsides would have been left alone. The last remnants of the old-growth rain forest below 850 meters (3,000 feet) were cleared by the mid-1970s, and the cycle of human poverty and population growth was maintained for another generation. An ever-increasing number of workers left the plantations in search of land to farm on the slopes of the mountains.

During the period that the Philippines was an American colony, rain forests were cleared for commercial purposes: Logging rapidly extracted profits for American companies and allowed for the expansion of plantations. After World War II, when the Philippines became independent, logging increased at a greater rate under combined foreign and Filipino ownership. While logging firms reaped large profits, wages were too low to allow workers to break out of poverty, and the roads built by the loggers opened ever-larger areas to landless farmers. Taxes on logging that might have paid for reforestation, rural development, education, or other services were kept very low, so that few benefits flowed to the local inhabitants. During the 20-year administration of Ferdinand Marcos, logging concessions were given to his supporters and allies; 25-year concessions for up to 100,000 hectares often were sold for a fee of one peso per hectare (about ten cents per acre); taxes averaged 30 pesos for a cubic meter of logs valued at an average of 2,800 pesos. Ultimately, under this arrangement, the poor and the middle class subsidized the rich by bearing the costs of floods, droughts, erosion, siltation, and lack of education. Corruption came to be a large factor in logging; many logging companies were owned by politicians who sought to maximize their own profits by keeping taxes unreasonably low (and actual payments lower still), while ignoring the needs of the people in the regions they represented. On Negros, old-growth forest declined to about eight percent in the mid-1970s, to six percent by 1984, and to less than four percent in 1992. Today, this forest exists as tiny patches of montane and mossy rain forest near the tops of the mountains; old-growth lowland forest exists only as a few thin ribbons between the montane forest and the cleared lowlands. These patches and ribbons of forest now function as small islands of natural rain-forest habitat surrounded by a sea of impoverished people.

NEGROS ISLAND TODAY

Although there are currently several small cities on Negros Island where industry and commerce thrive, the population of the island today is predominantly rural and poor. The coast is a heavily populated strip, with large numbers of subsistence fisherfolk; although they may do some farming and other work, these people make their living primarily from what they catch in the sea. In recent years this has become increasingly difficult, both because their population has grown and because commercial boats, often from other countries, have taken an increasingly greater portion of the catch. Dynamite fishing, clearing of mangrove forest that provides a nursery for fish of many species, removal of corals for building material and decoration, and pollution and siltation from the land have all diminished the capacity of the reefs to produce. The cumulative threats to marine ecosystems now equal those on land.

Inland from the coast lies the richest land, the fertile lowlands of weathered volcanic soil that produce bumper crops of sugar cane. Although this land is the most productive for agriculture, it is remarkably thinly populated; most of the land is covered not by crops for local consumption, and not by small farms owned by the people who till the land, but by large haciendas owned by just a few people, producing an exported crop. Nearly all farmwork is still done by hand, and wages for unskilled workers remain very low. Because the global price for sugar has dropped, pressure to keep wages low is strong. In recent years, the landowners have shifted their efforts to exporting prawns to Japan. In the process, they often destroy the last of the mangrove swamps when they dig the ponds in which the prawns are raised. Because no new money is being invested in the sugar-cane industry, it is becoming more and more inefficient, with small processing plants more than 50 years old belching smoke over the countryside.

Further inland from the cane fields are large coconut plantations, where copra (dried coconut used to produce oil and some other products) is produced. Huge areas were planted when the global price of copra was high for several decades after World War II; a few landowners made large profits, but left behind a crop that now barely pays for its harvesting. Cattle and water buffalo graze beneath the coconuts, adding a bit to the economic value of the land. This region is more densely populated than the lowland plantation lands, with some small farmers growing vegetable crops for local sale.

Most of the lowlands are covered not by crops for local consumption, but by large haciendas.

Most sugar processing plants are old and inefficient, belching smoke over the countryside. This plant on Leyte is quite similar to those on Negros.

Dense populations of impoverished, land-less farmers live in logged-over areas in the steep middle elevations, burning their fields to clear them of logging debris and vegeta-tion. A family of two adults and six children lived for over five years in this house near Lake Balinsasayao on Negros Island.

Still further inland, on the slopes of the mountains, where the soil is too poor for sugar cane or too isolated for coconut plantations, are some of the most densely inhabited parts of the island. At least 30 percent of the population lives in these upland areas, often making their clearings in second-growth forest left by logging operations in the 1970s and 1980s. Although neighbors respect each other's "own-ership" of the land they farm, they occupy the land illegally and live in constant fear of being forced from their only source of livelihood. They are called *kaingineros,* people who make slash-and-burn clearings, but they are generally unable to shift from one spot to another, as was done tradi-tionally, for there is often no place to which they may move. Most families live in huts made of thin planks and bamboo, more than a kilometer from the nearest road and often hundreds of meters from fresh water. They are almost always impoverished, earning only a few hundred dollars or less per year. The young men often labor in the cane fields or coconut plantations when there is work; they will also cut any trees that remain and use a water buffalo to haul the timbers to the nearest road for sale to a local businessman—often, in our experience, a close relative of a prominent local politician. Opportunities for education are seriously inadequate, and health care is distant and, for these people, often prohibitively expensive. Birth rates in this portion of the population are the highest for the nation, with an average family size over six and a growth rate of 2.8 percent per year or more.

As the children mature, it is rare for them to have a livelihood open to them other than to marry as soon as possible—for one person alone can do almost nothing—and move to the edge of the forest, either on Negros or on another island, where they clear a patch of farmland still higher on the mountain. On Negros, new farms are now cleared in areas well over 1,000 meters elevation where rainfall exceeds three meters per year and where the slope of the farmed land often exceeds 45° and rarely drops under 20°. When we talked with these farmers, they told us that they would prefer that no one move upslope from them because of the floods, erosion, and drought that will follow, but more than anything else they respect the need of their neighbors to survive. As more people move upslope, those below them become increasingly impoverished by the declining productivity of their land, and eventually have little choice but to move still higher on the mountain or to

another island, perpetuating the cycle. The land the *kaingineros* leave behind is soon covered only by tough, nearly useless sawgrass, which thrives in the fires that sweep across the hills as farmers clear their fields during each dry season. On Negros, as in most parts of the Philippines, 20 to 30 percent of the land is now covered by sawgrass—easily eroded and productive only for limited grazing for a few weeks each year.

Today, landless farmers continue to creep higher up the slopes into the little patches of remaining high-elevation rain forest on Negros; the unpopulated land that remains is steep, cold, and rainy, but may suffice for a few years for people who seek only survival. Many people emigrate to Mindanao and Palawan, but it is our impression that emigration is lower than the birth rate, and density continues to increase. It is the intense pressure from such people that now poses the greatest single threat to the survival of biodiversity on the island. Unless socio-economic changes that alter the cycle of poverty are instituted, destruction of the last forest looms within the next decade.

Accessible areas at middle elevation are converted to corn fields after logging debris is burned, even on slopes of 45 degrees or greater. Trees are cut on higher slopes nearby, and hauled out by water buffalo to the nearest road, for sale to owners of local lumber stores. Only the highest, most distant ridges retain old-growth forest.

THE HUMAN COSTS

Although the history of deforestation differs in its details in each part of the Philippines, the primary processes seen in the case of Negros are present nationwide. On all of the islands, human population density was originally low, but was influenced by outside forces to undergo tremendous growth. Natural resources, especially timber, have been viewed as a source of quick profits by a small group. No one considered the economic costs of exploitation. The export of raw agricultural products (whether sugar, tobacco, cotton, or hemp) depended on keeping wages at the lowest level possible, which in turn promoted a continued, rapid increase in population size. Subsidies, either direct (in the case of sugar) or indirect (through unreason-

In many areas on Negros Island, there is virtually no original vegetation remaining. After subsistence farmers move on, the middle slopes (roughly 500 to 1,000 meters) are covered by nearly useless sawgrass, and the lower slopes (200 to 500 meters) are covered by unproductive coconut groves. Steep slopes are often heavily eroded.

ably low taxes on logging and mining), have made the situation worse by causing marginal areas to be farmed, logged, or mined. These areas are often those that are most vulnerable because of steepness of their terrain, unusually shallow soils, or other factors. The surging population of impoverished, poorly educated people guaranteed profits for owners of plantations, but also drove people to the upland subsistence farming that now threatens the little rain forest that remains. At least 20 million Filipinos—about 30 percent of the population of 72 million—now live in rural upland areas, eking out a living from steep, wet, easily eroded lands. Migration between islands long served as a safety valve, but it is clear that the islands have now virtually reached their long-term carrying capacity.

One of the worst economic consequences of rain-forest destruction is erosion. Erosion under old-growth forest averages about three metric tons per hectare per year, whether in the lowlands or high mountains. In the lowlands where the terrain is relatively flat, erosion under second-growth forest increases to 12 tons, and in open grasslands it reaches an average of 84 tons. But the worst erosion occurs on slopes of up to 60° at elevations over 1,000 meters that have been cleared and then farmed. In these areas, erosion can often exceed 250 tons per hectare per year—five times what most agricultural economists consider to be the maximum acceptable level. Such erosion can reduce soil fertility by 30 to 70 percent.

These costs climb vastly higher when the effects of siltation and flooding downstream are considered. Although virtually no national figures are available, the huge plumes of muddy water reaching out to sea from nearly every river give clear testimony to the impact of siltation on coral reefs. Dams built for irrigation and hydroelectric power are being filled with silt two to three times faster than expected. For example, a dam built in the Magat watershed in northern Luzon in 1982 to supply water for one of the largest irrigated areas in the country was originally designed to have a functional lifetime of 95 years, but heightened erosion due to clearing of forest has reduced the dam's lifetime to 40 years at most.

The flooding itself is often terribly destructive. The flood in Naga City described in the first chapter of this book killed several people and did great damage to the region, but it was by no means unusually severe among the steadily increasing floods in recent years.

The worst flood on record struck Ormoc City on Leyte on 7 November 1991, when a typhoon swept over a mountainside that had been severely over-logged in the previous several years. Our team had conducted studies on Leyte about 50 kilometers south of Ormoc City in 1984 and 1987, and often went into the city to buy supplies. As we drove past the heavily denuded mountainsides, we were incredulous that anyone could see such devastation and not be worried about the potential for disaster. According to official statistics, 100 percent of the watershed had been cleared, nearly all of it planted with sugar cane on plantations owned by six families, with the largest holdings belonging to the family of the mayor. When a typhoon struck directly (one of an average of five that hit the area each year), water in the two rivers that flow through the city rose ten feet in three hours. About 7,000 people died (many bodies were never recovered, so the count is uncertain); in one section of the city, only 200 of the 2,500 residents survived. Most of the city was severely damaged; the main coastal highway and bridges were destroyed; agricultural crops were devastated by erosion or covered by mud; and the fertile Ormoc Bay was filled with muddy water.

A year after that terrible flood, no reforestation had taken place, and no flood-control plans were in place. A city councilor said at that time: "We are still waiting for a plan for reforestation that will not disrupt the economy. To make reforestation attractive, the landowners must be convinced that the economic value of the trees will be commensurate to the value of the sugar cane."

Floods in Butuan City, Manila, and Aparri in recent years have demonstrated that removing the rain forest cover—whether for logging, subsistence farms, or plantations—is having increasingly severe impact. The intensification of storms associated with the El Niño effect is making the problem worse, but it is deforestation that has allowed the damage to occur.

Once the rainwaters have flooded down the denuded slopes instead of entering the groundwater system, they are no longer available to feed the rivers during the dry months. The area of agricultural land in the country affected by drought expanded from 812 square kilometers in 1968 to almost 14,000 square kilometers in 1987, and has continued to increase. In 1992, drought conditions that were widely blamed on over-logging struck over 2,300 square kilometers of prime agricultural land in various

After its watershed was logged and converted to sugar-cane plantations, Ormoc City suffered a flood that killed 7,000 people and severely damaged homes, businesses, and roads.

is backed by a 78-square-kilometer mountainside watershed that averages 30° slope. In 1985, forest covered over half of the watershed; in the forest, erosion averaged 0.6 tons per hectare per year, but in logged areas it averaged 141 tons. From May to December 1986, after logging expanded, 49,080 tons of logging-associated sediment washed into

the bay, resulting in the death of about 50 percent of the corals in the reef closest to the mouth of the Bacuit River. Economic estimates made at the time projected fisheries revenues of about $28 million and tourism revenues of about $25 million over ten years without logging. These numbers were expected to drop to about $15 million and $6 million, respectively, with logging. The logging itself would produce about $8.5 million if carried out, but nothing, of course, if it were terminated. The net of these three primary commercial sectors for the Bacuit Bay area thus is about $43 million without logging, and $29.5 million with logging. The difference of $13.5 million represents a loss to the local economy. The estimates also noted that, after the ten-year period, ecotourism and fishing could continue indefinitely, but the logging could resume at most only every 20 to 50 years, and perhaps not ever again.

For the inhabitants of the areas below the steep, wet terrain covered by rain forest, deforestation is usually a losing proposition. Economic development in the Philippines is badly needed, but protection of vulnerable watersheds and marine habitats is a crucial component of sustainable development. Logging in steep areas does not produce net benefit—it produces a net loss.

Commercial logging in the Philippines now usually results in a net economic loss due to damage to agriculture, fisheries, businesses, and roads, partly because of increased floods and droughts downstream. Erosion often leaves behind only denuded, barren limestone.

parts of the country. On Panay, where deforestation is among the worst in the nation, 450 square kilometers of such land were affected, accounting for the loss of 118,000 tons of rice alone. Official assistance was limited only to farmers suffering 90 to 100 percent damage; the others (about two-thirds of the total suffering serious damage) were left to fend for themselves. Many rural families survived by making charcoal from stands of remnant forest, further accentuating the underlying problem. In Iloilo City, the largest city on the island, only two percent of the watershed was forested in 1992 (and it is less today); during the drought, water was available in the city only four days per week, from four a.m. to seven p.m. From the Cagayan River valley in the north to the Agusan River valley in the south, many areas have had similar droughts in recent years, and newspapers cite their increasing frequency and intensity.

In addition to the direct costs of damage caused by deforestation, the indirect loss of income can be great as well, as shown clearly by the example of northern Palawan Island. The 120-square-kilometer Bacuit Bay, with the adjacent resort town of El Nido, is the site of an active ecotourism business based on the beautiful coral reefs of the region; the seas also provide livelihood to numerous subsistence fisherfolk. The bay

THE BIOLOGICAL COSTS

Prior to 1996, discussions of endangered mammals rarely mentioned the Philippines. The *Red Data Book*, the official listing of endangered species by the IUCN, was intended to be based on purely objective criteria, but since large mammals are much better known than small mammals, large species were most likely to be listed. For a country like the Philippines, whose relatively poorly known fauna consists of mostly small mammals, it is not surprising that few species were listed, aside from the tamaraw and a few other conspicuous species.

However, in 1996 a new edition of the *Red Data Book* was published based on a new effort to examine all species equally, incorporating all of the new information gathered in the past decade of intensive research in many tropical countries, including the Philippines. The result was staggering: A full quarter of all known species of mammals—1,100 out of the world total of 4,500—were listed as threatened to some significant degree. From the Philippines, 49 species were included, enough to place the country seventh world-wide in number of threatened mammals.

But the greater shock came when the sizes of the countries were factored in. First on the list were the giant nations—Brazil, Australia, China, the United States—but when corrected for size (that is, when the countries were compared on an acre-for-acre basis), the Philippines vaulted to the top of the list. When size of the countries is considered, there are more endangered species of mammals in the Philippines than in any other place in the world.

When we look at the distribution of endangered mammals (see map at right), a pattern quickly becomes apparent. In each of the faunal regions, which are defined by the Ice-Age islands and land-bridges within the Philippines, a substantial portion of its unique species is endangered; there is no place in the Philippines that has been exempt from the forces of destruction. Little Sibuyan Island, on which we found five new species of mammals, has three endangered species—two of which are among the new species we discovered; on tiny Camiguin we discovered two new species, one of which was already endangered at the time we found it. About 24 percent of the unique species of Greater Luzon and Greater Mindanao are endangered; on

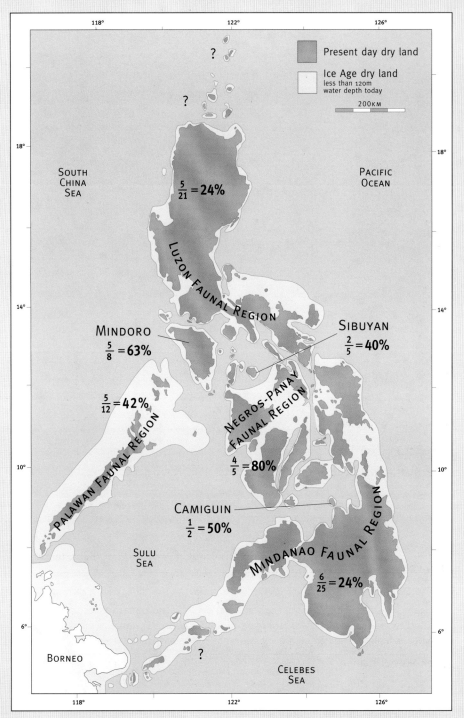

DISTRIBUTION OF ENDANGERED MAMMALS

Present day dry land

Ice Age dry land
less than 120m
water depth today

200 KM

SOUTH CHINA SEA

PACIFIC OCEAN

LUZON FAUNAL REGION
$\frac{5}{21}$ = 24%

MINDORO
$\frac{5}{8}$ = 63%

SIBUYAN
$\frac{2}{5}$ = 40%

$\frac{5}{12}$ = 42%

NEGROS-PANAY FAUNAL REGION
$\frac{4}{5}$ = 80%

PALAWAN FAUNAL REGION

CAMIGUIN
$\frac{1}{2}$ = 50%

MINDANAO FAUNAL REGION
$\frac{6}{25}$ = 24%

SULU SEA

BORNEO

CELEBES SEA

Updated and redrawn from Heaney, 1993.

As a result of habitat destruction, all of the faunal regions in the Philippines have endangered species of unique mammals. Between 24 and 80 percent of the total unique species present in each faunal region are endangered. (For some areas, we have no current information.) Taken together, about 50 mammal species are currently threatened with extinction, making the Philippine fauna one of the most severely endangered in the world.

Mindoro and Greater Negros-Panay, the proportions are 63 percent and 80 percent, respectively. Individually, these figures rank among the highest of any faunal region worldwide. Collectively, they paint an unparalleled picture of approaching extinction.

A look at the map of remaining old-growth rain forest in the Philippines (see page 63) provides a likely explanation: The less rain forest that remains in a given region, the greater the proportion of endangered species of mammals. Deforestation has destroyed the habitat of the animals, reducing their populations to a fraction of their original sizes. The tiny sizes of the populations are reason enough for concern because of the rising potential for inbreeding problems, but perhaps more importantly, as small populations decline in size they are increasingly vulnerable to complete destruction by periodic storms, droughts, floods, disease, or other factors such as the occasional failure of a fruit crop in a small area of rain forest. They are also much more susceptible to extinction by hunters, because they cannot hide effectively when their patch of habitat can be crossed by a man with a dog in just a few hours or less. Tiny populations are nearly always teetering on the brink of extinction.

From our studies of the distribution patterns of mammals in the Philippines, we know that reducing the area of habitat nearly always results in the extinction of species. The clearest example comes from our field work on some of the islands that made up Greater Mindanao. Over a ten-year period, our teams inventoried the mammals on Mindanao and a series of four smaller islands: Leyte, Bohol, Biliran, and Maripipi; the smallest of these is only 22 square kilometers. We chose them because, when we did our surveys, all still had fairly extensive tracts of old-growth rain forest from near sea level to the mountaintops. All of these islands were part of Greater Mindanao until about 10,000 years ago (which is a brief moment in geological terms), and all share a virtually identical mammal fauna, in all respects but one. Mindanao has the largest number of species of native, non-flying mammals, 25. Leyte, which is one-tenth the size of Mindanao, has 15. Biliran, which is about one-tenth the size of Leyte, has 12 species, and Maripipi, about one-tenth the size of Biliran, has seven. (Bohol, with 13 species and about the same size as Leyte,

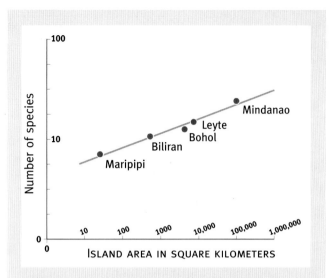

The number of species of mammals (excluding bats and non-native species) on islands that once were part of Greater Mindanao is highly correlated with the size of the islands. A decline in habitat area is almost always associated with a decline in biological diversity.

From Rickart et al. (1993) and unpublished data.

was added just for good measure.) There are no unique species on any of the smaller islands; they all have a reduced set of the species also found on Mindanao.

As shown in the figure at the top of this page, when we plot the number of species against land area for each of the six islands, a remarkably strong correlation between area and number of species becomes clear. In spite of their common biological and geological history, and the generally identical nature of their faunas, the smaller islands have fewer species—and the smaller the island, the smaller the number of species. The message is unmistakable: At the end of the Ice Age, when rising water broke apart Greater Mindanao, many species were unable to survive as the islands became isolated and shrank. Shrinking local populations led to natural extinction. Analysis of our data on the ecology of the animals shows that the species most vulnerable to extinction were those whose population densities were naturally low, those that lived only in a single type of habitat, and those that were unable to tolerate any habitat other than undisturbed old-growth forest.

The less rain forest that remains in a given region, the greater the proportion of endangered species.

Like most unique species of animals and plants in the Philippines, the Philippine eagle depends on old-growth rain forest for its survival.

Look again at the map of current forest cover in the Philippines (page 63). The natural habitat on most islands has been reduced, but it has also been divided into tiny isolated islands of forest habitat surrounded by a sea of humans. Our studies of mammals on the islands of Greater Mindanao leads us to predict that the mammals (and other species) in these forest patches are now vulnerable to extinction due to the shrinking of their habitat. Studies of mammal species in forest reserves in the United States, East Africa, and elsewhere tell us that this prediction is probably correct, and the correlation between the percentage of endangered species and the amount of forest cover makes the prediction virtually certain. As the rain forests of the Philippines shrink, more and more species are being stressed to the point of extinction by lack of habitat and tiny population size.

There are dozens of examples of such cases. On Mindoro, where only eight percent of the original rain forest was left in 1992, we see the tamaraw, a shrew, three unusual rodent species, and at least two fruit bats listed in the 1997 *Philippine Red Data Book* (which supplements and expands the IUCN list) among those critically threatened. On Negros, where primary forest cover is down to less than four percent, we see the severely endangered Visayan spotted deer, with perhaps no more than 200 left in the wild, and the Philippine tube-nosed fruit bat, which is probably down to one percent of its original population, barely surviving in a narrow band of lowland forest around a few mountain peaks. Illegal logging and clearing for subsistence farms cuts that forest band ever thinner. In some cases, the damage is greater, sadly definitive, and irreversible. The Philippine bare-backed fruit bat is now

The exquisite

Cebu flower-

pecker is proba-

bly the most

endangered

species of bird

in the world,

with only four

individuals

known to be

alive.

extinct, one of the first species to verify the horrible prediction of impending extinction for one-third to two-thirds of the species of mammals unique to the Philippines.

The picture for birds is similarly bleak. Of the 172 species of birds that are unique to the Philippines, 75 are listed as endangered. All but one of the 172 endemic species, and all of the 75 endangered species, depend on forest for their survival, and many on undisturbed rain forest. The Philippines is the only country in the world to be entirely covered by the Endemic Bird Areas (EBAs) recognized by Birdlife International. Three of these EBAs in the central Philippines are among the ten highest-priority conservation areas for birds world-wide. The Philippines has the third-highest number of globally threatened bird species (after Indonesia and Brazil, which are more than 20 times larger), and has the most endangered and critically endangered unique bird species (40). Again we see clear evidence that the number and percentage of bird species that are threatened is proportional to the amount of destruction of old-growth forest within each region. Cebu, for example, which is the most thoroughly deforested island in the country—it has almost no native vegetation remaining—had 14 species and subspecies of birds that are (or were) found nowhere else in the world. Three of these are now extinct, and all but one of those still living are believed

to number fewer than 100 individuals. One of these, the exquisite Cebu flowerpecker, is probably the most endangered species of bird in the world, with only four individuals known to be alive. The destruction of rain-forest habitat may have doomed these birds, just as it has caused Cebu City, the second-largest city in the Philippines, to ration water and to suffer increasingly from salt-water contamination of wells due to the lack of rainwater entering the groundwater system.

Birds and mammals are the best-known groups of organisms in the world; for other creatures, so little is known that global comparison of numbers of endangered species is not possible. However, as the *Philippine Red Data Book* published in 1997 demonstrates, there are endangered reptiles, amphibians, and butterflies in many parts of the country, and a wide range of sources document the ever-increasing numbers of plant species endangered by habitat destruction and over-harvesting.

Taken together, these data form the basis for Conservation International's recent description of the Philippines as having the most severely endangered plant and animal communities on earth. Other, much larger countries may have more endangered species and patches of forest, but nowhere are the problems more intense and proportionately more significant.

Decisions made today will make the difference between tragedy and prosperity. For some species, and some watersheds, it is already too late.

Prospects for Recovery

LAWRENCE R. HEANEY

THE CASE FOR HOPE

Plotting a corrective course for a country with such severe social and environmental problems as the Philippines is an enormous challenge. The damage has been substantial, and the extent of change required to turn the system from one of approaching disaster to one of long-term stability is daunting. However, many aspects of the decline that began long ago have been either reversed or at least slowed.

One of the greatest problems has been a paucity of accurate and current information on wildlife, forests, and the environment in the Philippines. This is changing rapidly; newspapers now avidly cover stories about floods, droughts, and deforestation, and bring corrupt practices to light. Information is gradually making its way into grade-school and high-school curricula, and books about nature and wild animals and plants are being published frequently; for example, the Philippines now has the best field guide to marine mammals of any country in Southeast Asia, and the new *Philippine Red Data Book* is one of the first comprehensive listings of endangered species for a developing country.

When I began doing field work in the Philippines in 1981, there were perhaps a half-dozen active Filipino researchers studying wild mammals, birds, reptiles, and amphibians; at the time, there was virtually no funding to support such research; speaking or writing about environmental issues of any sort was likely to result in harrassment and intimidation, loss of employment, and occasionally worse. In 1991, with funding from the MacArthur Foundation through The Field Museum, a program for training and field research was established for young Filipino field biologists, and the Wildlife Conservation Society of the Philippines was founded. The level of interest in wildlife research has grown dramatically since then; attendance has gone from about 25 at the first meeting to over 175 at recent meetings, many of the participants enthusiastic graduate students who are doing excellent field studies. The mem-

Protecting the remaining old-growth rain forest is essential for both biological and economic stability.

bers of the society work together to conduct research, promote knowledge and training, and act as the primary conduits for getting new information about biodiversity to the public.

For some of the most severely endangered species, integrated programs of field studies and captive breeding of conspicuous "flagship" species have been established. Although captive breeding will never provide the stability that comes with successful protection of the natural habitat, such programs provide thousands of Filipinos with personal contact with endangered native species every year, raise awareness about environmental problems, and keep alive the possibility of re-introducing endangered species into the wild once conditions in former habitat improve. One of the most successful of these programs involves the Visayan spotted deer; although wild populations continue to dwindle, the captive herd now numbers well over 100 individuals and is growing rapidly. With gradual improvement in conditions on the mountains of Negros, the prospect of release of some captive animals into the beautiful area around Lake Balinsasayao seems to be approaching rapidly. Captive-breeding programs for the giant fruit bats, endangered wild pigs, and some other species are also contributing to conservation in various parts of the country. Unfortunately, the older and larger projects—especially those for the tamaraw and the Philippine eagle—remain mired in controversy and have yet to produce a positive result. In all cases, protection of wild populations ought to be the top priority, especially since these large species provide one of the best sources of public support for protecting the rain forest.

Captive breeding of endangered species of giant fruit bats, Visayan spotted deer, and other species provides important new information and opportunities for public education, but protection of natural habitat remains the only hope for the great majority of endangered species. Photographs taken at Silliman University, Dumaguete City.

One of the most positive signs in the past six to eight years has been the rejuvenation of the system of national parks and other protected areas. During the Marcos years, none of the parks received meaningful protection, and many were partially logged by companies holding permits for logging on their boundaries; several parks were almost entirely clear-cut. Several internationally funded park management projects are now under way, after assessment studies that began in 1989. Beginning in 1994, the Global Environmental Facility of the World Bank provided funding for management, protection, and community development at ten sites, and in 1996 the European Union provided funding for eight additional sites (most of which are rain forest, some are marine). Additional funding for similar projects has come from the Danish and Dutch governments.

Equally important, the Philippine government has moved actively in the past several years to declare new national parks and other protected areas in critical regions, including Mount Kitanglad in northern Mindanao, the mountainous cores of Sibuyan and Camiguin islands, and the Northern Sierra Madre Wilderness Park in northeastern Luzon, now the largest national park in the country. Although new parks and greatly improved protection activities are badly needed, there has been remarkable progress. One especially positive aspect of the new national park system is that it is gradually being shaped to provide protected areas in every biogeographical region in the country. The Philippines may soon be one of the first countries in the world to have a park system that is specifically designed to safeguard biological diversity. The primary challenges for the park system currently are to increase coverage of the lowland dipterocarp forest, which has been the habitat most severely decimated in recent decades; to find constructive, effective ways of drawing poor farmers out of the parks; and to bring an end to the illegal logging that continues to occur in most of the parks.

In a country as poor as the Philippines, economic growth is essential to solving environmental problems; as long as a majority of the population (in this case, about 60 percent) is composed of people in rural areas who live below the poverty level, the fight to protect forest is likely to be a losing battle. One of the most encouraging signs for the Philippines has been a strongly expanding economy; from 1995 to 1997, the economy grew by about 14.5 percent. After the onset of the Asian economic downturn that

Two areas on Bohol photographed near Bilan in 1987, just five kilometers apart and both logged in the early 1960s, show the benefits of reforestation and forest protection. At right, a logged-over area that remained unprotected was farmed for several years and is now barren and dry. Above, reforestation with the fast-growing legume called ipil-ipil (Leucena) provided shade, allowing natural vegetation to recover, and protection from logging by government agencies produced a functioning watershed, as well as habitat for recovering populations of native mammals and birds.

began in late 1997, the Philippines was still projected to have the strongest economic growth during 1998 in all of Southeast Asia, but that seems increasingly uncertain. The recent economic growth stands in contrast to the majority of the Marcos era and its immediate aftermath, when the rate of economic growth was less than the rate of population growth in all but a few years, actually shrinking by about 14.5 percent from 1980 to 1991 while the population grew by about 2.5 percent per year.

All of the steps described here are necessary for substantive, long-term improvement, but even taken together they do not offer a complete solution to the problem. This is because they do not address its root—poverty. The Philippine socio-economic system continues to emphasize opportunity for the well-to-do at the expense of the poor, either directly or indirectly. Although the current economic growth is a good sign, there is reason for concern about its long-term impact. From 1992 to 1997, most of the increased income went to the top ten percent of the income-earners in the country; the bottom 50 percent actually lost ground because of increases in prices. Until the conditions that promote the continuance of rural poverty are changed, the root

causes of environmental destruction will remain. Meaningful change requires effective rural development programs, fair and equitable taxation and subsidy programs, and management of natural resources in a manner that specifically requires that all segments of society benefit fairly. These must be coupled with policies that promote economic growth, industrialization, and urbanization, with the inevitable attendant increase in education and decrease in birth rates. These are the only means likely to help the Philippines bring about true sustainable development and avoid the looming social and environmental catastrophe.

RETURN TO MOUNT ISAROG

The last sounds we heard on Mount Isarog in 1988 were birds singing, cicadas buzzing, and chain saws roaring. As the Philippines sought to redefine itself after the 1986 revolution that deposed Ferdinand Marcos, conditions in the countryside hardly could have looked worse. Armed conflict between several rebel groups and the military was common, the economy was in tatters, poverty was increasing dramatically, government was in disarray (with coups attempted several times each year), and local "warlords" often operated with impunity. On Mount Isarog, the national park seemed to be viewed as a no-man's land, open to anyone willing to exploit it.

But when Marcos was deposed, people gradually became aware that they could speak up and influence local events with much less fear of violent reprisal. Newspapers began to publish more detailed and critical analyses of local events, identifying corruption and mismanagement in gov-

ernment and business. International aid agencies that had virtually abandoned the Philippines because of government corruption and repression returned quickly, and began to help the Filipino people turn things around.

In 1990, several international agencies worked together with the Philippine government to arrange a "debt-for-nature swap," in which old unpaid loans to the Philippine government from foreign banks were paid by the international agencies at a discounted rate, in return for a promise to spend a portion of the value of the loan (in this case, several million dollars) on revitalizing the national park system.

A small part of this funding went to the Haribon Foundation, one of the very few conservation groups that had remained active and vocal during the Marcos years. With this funding, Haribon initiated a small program in 1990 in the communities surrounding Mount Isarog to help the poor farmers in the area—thousands of whom lived within the boundaries of the park—develop a basic understanding of forest ecology, environmental economics, and park management. It also provided the tools to help translate the conceptual issues into practical action: Local people were given paralegal training, taught how to run community meetings, and instructed in how to write proposals for

further funding. The program also informed people about the new national constitution, which delegated much authority for resource management to local communities.

The results of the program were apparent by 1992. A proposal from the community to a Finnish funding source led to a grant to reforest many of the areas of sawgrass on the mountain slopes that had once been rain forest. The reforestation would provide fuelwood to lessen impact on the remaining rain forest, help control erosion and flooding, and eventually provide a source of building materials. A grant from the Foundation for the Philippine Environment established an "alternative livelihoods project" that allowed former loggers and slash-and-burn farmers to switch to less destructive means of living. Intensive vegetable farming, livestock raising, and small crafts flourished as a result.

The community, without outside funding, also established a group of forest guards to control illegal logging in the rain forest; the members would simply talk with the loggers and try to convince them to stop, although the forest guards were also deputized by the Department of Environment and Natural Resources to confiscate chain saws and any other materials used in illegal logging. Because most of the remaining loggers were coming from outside the local communities, the communities passed ordinances against transporting lumber on the community roads as another legal means to stop deforestation of the park.

In January and February of 1994, the issue of illegal logging came to a head. People from outside the local communities were being paid by a Naga City businessman to cut rain-forest trees on several parts of the mountain easily reached by road. Army personnel were hired to accompany the loggers and trucks—illegally but quite effectively. At this point, community leaders agreed that collective action was needed. One afternoon, after a small truck had gone up the mountain to pick up the latest load of lumber, a group met to erect a barricade. When the truck came back down and reached the barricade, over 50 people were present, including officials from the communities, members of the new community Environmental Paralegal Team (EPT), and other residents. When the driver and heavily armed men in the truck were told that they were acting illegally and that the lumber and truck were being confiscated, they reacted angrily, destroying a portion of the barricade. Shots were fired, the crowd scattered, and the truck headed into town.

Not long after, on a nearby road that reached into the park, community officials, members of the EPT, and other residents stopped a small truck carrying logs from Mount Isarog without permits. Armed soldiers from the nearby Philippine Army camp arrived quickly, and forced the release of the truck and logs. Among the witnesses, several had two-way radios and described the scene to people in a nearby town, including newspaper reporters. Substantial publicity concerning the case followed, with the town mayor and Army garrison officers accused of involvement. The Environmental Paralegal Team filed lawsuits against several people, and was quickly met with offers of bribes and threats of reprisals. The lawsuits were eventually dismissed, principally because the regional government offices involved in park and forest management consistently failed to send representatives to court hearings. No one was arrested or fined, but the publicity and public outcry seemed to have an effect: The number of trucks going up the mountain, and the amount of illegal logging, declined, and remain low at the time of this writing.

Mount Isarog was recently selected as one of ten sites to receive funding for continued protection and community-development activities through a grant from the European Union. Salaries for forest guards (many of whom had been volunteer community forest guards) and a general supervisor will be paid through the grant. The park boundaries will be re-surveyed and marked clearly, and socio-economic research will identify progress and problems, and will seek new solutions.

For rural people in areas like Mount Isarog, the future looks uncertain. Poverty is severe, people are poorly educated, and past damage to the environment continues to cause floods and droughts. But economic activity in Naga City and other small urban centers is increasing, providing some jobs and increasing the market for the vegetables and livestock produced by small-scale farmers. Hikers and bird-watchers are beginning to visit the park, hiring guides and buying food from local restaurants. A sense of optimism and hope for the future is present in the people who live near the forest.

The future of biological diversity and human society are tightly intertwined in the Philippines. Massive extinction and economic instability and decline are both almost certain outcomes without the rain forests that provide habitat for a stunning array of plants and animals. These forests provide clean water and protection from floods, droughts, and erosion. Given the tiny amounts of forest that remain in most places in the nation, it is clear that the moment of crisis and decision is now upon us. The decisions made today will make the difference between tragedy and prosperity; in ten years, perhaps in one year, and perhaps even tomorrow, it will be too late. For some species, and some watershed forests, it is already too late; some species are extinct, and some islands have no remaining natural forest. The greatest treasure of the Philippine rain forest, the one most worthy of protecting and guarding jealously, is the forest itself. There is still time to assure a prosperous future for most of the people of the Philippines and most of the remarkable fauna that is their natural heritage, and to prevent irreparable environmental damage—but there is not much time, and it is slipping away.

The greatest treasure of the Philippine rain forest is the forest itself.

BIBLIOGRAPHY

Alcala, A.C. 1976. *Philippine Land Vertebrates*. New Day Publishers, Quezon City. 176 pp.

Alcala, A.C. 1986. *Guide to the Philippine Flora and Fauna. Vol. 10, Amphibians and Reptiles*. Natural Resources Management Centre and University of the Philippines, Manila.

Alcala, A.C., and C.C. Custodio. 1997. Status of endemic Philippine amphibians. *Sylvatrop* (1995) 5: 72–86.

Asis, C.V. 1971. *Plants of the Philippines*. Science Education Center, University of the Philippines, Quezon City. 512 pp.

Baille, J., and B. Groombridge. 1996. *1996 IUCN Red List of Threatened Animals*. International Union for the Conservation of Nature, Gland. 368 pp.

Balete, D.S., H.C. Miranda, L.R. Heaney, and J.F. Rieger. 1992. Diversity and conservation of Philippine land vertebrates: An annotated bibliography. *Silliman Journal* 36: 129–149.

Balete, D.S., and L.R. Heaney. 1998. Density, biomass, and movement estimates for murid rodents in mossy forest on Mount Isarog, southern Luzon, Philippines. *Ecotropica* 3: (in press).

Bibby, C.J., N.J. Collar, M.J. Crosby, M.F. Heath, C. Imboden, T.H. Johnson, A.J. Long, A.J. Statterfield, and S.J. Thirgood. 1992. *Putting Biodiversity on the Map: Priority areas for global conservation*. International Council for Bird Preservation, Cambridge. 90 pp.

Braatz, S. 1992. *Conserving Biological Diversity: A strategy for protected areas in the Asia-Pacific region*. World Bank Technical Paper Number 193: 1–66.

Broad, R., and J. Cavanagh. 1993. *Plundering Paradise: The struggle for the environment in the Philippines*. University of California Press, Berkeley. 197 pp.

Brown, W.C. 1997. Biogeography of amphibians in the islands of the Southwest Pacific. *Proceedings of the California Academy of Sciences* 50: 21–38.

Brown, W.C., and A.C. Alcala. 1978. *Philippine Lizards of the Family Gekkonidae*. Silliman University, Dumaguete City. 146 pp.

Brown, W.C., and A.C. Alcala. 1980. *Philippine Lizards of the Family Scincidae*. Silliman University, Dumaguete City. 264 pp.

Brown, W.C. and A.C. Alcala. 1994. Philippine frogs of the family Rhacophoridae. *Proceedings of the California Academy of Sciences* 48: 185–220.

Brown, W.C. and E.L. Alcala. 1995. A new species of *Brachymeles* (Reptilia: Scincidae) from Catanduanes Island, Philippines. *Proceedings of the Biological Society of Washington* 108: 392–94.

Brown, W.H. 1919. *Vegetation of Philippine Mountains*. Monograph of the Bureau of Science, Manila, 13: 1–434.

Christensen, T.D., and T. Lund. 1993. *A comparison of the avian communities in different forest types in the northern Sierra Madre Mountains, the Philippines*. Unpubl. M.Sc. Thesis, Zoological Museum, University of Copenhagen, Denmark. Vols. 1 & 2, 63 + 72 pp.

Collar, N.J., M.J. Crosby, and A.J. Stattersfield. 1994. Birds to watch 2. *Birdlife Conservation* Series 4: 407. Birdlife International, Cambridge.

Curio, E. 1993. Report on bird species recorded during a (preliminary) Philippines conservation expedition, 3 July – 26 August 1993. Unpubl. report, Bochum, 32 pp.

Custodio, C.C., M.V. Lepiten, and L.R. Heaney. 1996. *Bubalus mindorensis. Mammalian Species* 520: 1–5.

Danielsen, F., D.S. Balete, T.D. Christensen, M. Heegaard, O.F. Jakobsen, A. Jensen, T. Lund, and M.K. Poulsen. 1994. *Conservation of Biological Diversity in the Sierra Madre Mountains of Isabela and Southern Cagayan Province, the Philippines*. BirdLife International, Manila and Copenhagen. 146 pp.

Delacour, J., and E. Mayr. 1946. *Birds of the Philippines*. MacMillan Co., New York. 309 pp.

Developmental Alternatives, Inc. 1992. *An Aerial Reconnaissance of Closed Canopy Forests*. Natural Resources Management Program, Manila. 71 pp.

Dickinson, E.C., R.S. Kennedy, and K.C. Parkes. 1991. *The Birds of the Philippines: An annotated checklist*. British Ornithologists Union, Tring. 507 pp.

DuPont, J.E. 1971. *Philippine Birds*. Delaware Museum of Natural History, Greenville. 480 pp.

Evans, T.D., G.C.L. Dutson, and T.M. Brooks. *Cambridge Philippines Rainforest Project 1991, Final Report*. Birdlife International, Cambridge. 96 pp.

Fairbanks, R.G. 1989. A 17,000-year glacio-eustatic sea level record: Influence of glacial melting on the Younger Dryas event and deep-sea circulation. *Nature* 342: 637–642.

Ferner, J.W., R.M. Brown, and A.E. Greer. 1997. A new genus and species of moist closed canopy forest skinks from the Philippines. *Journal of Herpetology* 31: 187–92.

Fooden, J. 1991. Systematic review of Philippine macaques (Primates, Cercopithecidae: *Macaca fascicularis* subspp.). *Fieldiana: Zoology* (n.s.) 64: 1–44.

Fooden, J. 1995. Systematic review of Southeast Asian longtail macaques, *Macaca fascicularis* (Raffles, [1821]). *Fieldiana: Zoology* (n.s.) 81: 1–206.

Fuller, M., R. McCabe, I.S. Williams, J. Almaco, R.Y. Encina, A.S. Zanoria, and J.A. Wolfe. 1983. Paleomagnetism of Luzon, pp. 79–84. *In* Hayes, D.E., ed., *The Tectonic and Geologic Evolution of South-east Asian Seas and Islands: Part 2*. American Geophysical Union Monograph 27: 1–396.

Gamalinda, E., and S. Coronel (eds.). 1993. *Saving the Earth: The Philippine Experience* (Third Ed.). Philippine Center for Investigative Journalism, Makati. 203 pp.

Gonzales, P.C. 1983. Birds of Catanduanes. *Zoological Papers. National Museum Manila* 2: 1–125.

Gonzales, P.C., and C.P. Rees. 1988. *Birds of the Philippines*. Haribon Foundation for the Conservation of Natural Resources, Manila. 184 pp.

Goodman, S.M., and P.C. Gonzales. 1990. The birds of Mt. Isarog National Park, southern Luzon, Philippines, with particular reference to altitudinal distribution. *Fieldiana: Zoology* (n.s.) 60: 1–39.

Goodman, S.M., and N.R. Ingle. 1993. Sibuyan Island in the Philippines: threatened and in need of conservation. *Oryx* 27: 174–80.

Goodman, S.M., D.E. Willard, and P.C. Gonzales. 1995. The birds of Sibuyan Island, Romblon Province, Philippines, with particular reference to elevational distribution and biogeographic affinities. *Fieldiana: Zoology* (n.s.) 82: 1–57.

Groombridge, B. (Ed.). 1992. *Global Biodiversity: Status of the Earth's Living Resources*. Chapman and Hall, London. 585 pp.

Guzman, E. de, R.M. Umali, and E.D. Sotalbo. 1986. Philippine dipterocarps. In *Guide to Philippine Flora and Fauna* III: 1–74.

Guzman, E. de, and E.S. Fernando. 1986. Philippine palms. In *Guide to Philippine Flora and Fauna* IV: 147–254.

Hall, R., and D. Blundell eds., 1996. Reconstructing Cenozoic SE Asia, pp. 153–184. *In* Tectonic Evolution of Southeast Asia. *Geological Society Special Publications* 106: 1–566.

Hamilton, W. 1979. Tectonics of the Indonesian Region. *Geological Survey Professional Papers* 1078: 1–345.

Harper, P., and E.S. Peplow. 1991. *Philippines Handbook*. Moon Publications Inc., Chico. 587 pp.

Hashimoto, W. 1981. Geological development of the Philippines, pp. 83–170, and Supplementary notes on the geological history of the Philippines, pp. 171–192. *In* Kobiyashi, T., R. Toriyama, and W. Hashimoto, eds., *Geology and Palaeontology of Southeast Asia* 22: 1–192.

Heaney, L.R. 1986. Biogeography of mammals in Southeast Asia: Estimates of rates of colonization, extinction, and speciation. *Biological Journal of the Linnean Soc.*, 28: 127–165.

Heaney, L.R. 1991. An analysis of patterns of distribution and species richness among Philippine fruit bats (Pteropodidae). *Bulletin of the American Museum of Natural History* 206: 1–432.

Heaney, L.R. 1991. A synopsis of climatic and vegetational change in Southeast Asia. *Climatic Change* 19: 53–61.

Heaney, L.R. 1993. Biodiversity patterns and the conservation of mammals in the Philippines. *Asia Life Sciences* 2: 261–274.

Heaney, L.R., D.S. Balete, and A.T.L. Dans. 1997. Terrestrial mammals, pp. 116–144. *In* Wildlife Conservation Society of the Philippines, *Philippine Red Data Book*. Bookmark, Manila. 240 pp.

Heaney, L.R., D.S. Balete, L. Dolar, A.C. Alcala, A. Dans, P.C. Gonzales, N. Ingle, M. Lepiten, W. Oliver, E.A. Rickart, B.R. Tabaranza, Jr., and R.C.B. Utzurrum. A synopsis of the mammalian fauna of the Philippine Islands. *Fieldiana: Zoology* (in press).

Heaney, L.R., D.S. Balete, E.A. Rickart, R.C.B. Utzurrum, and P.C. Gonzales. Mammalian diversity on Mt. Isarog, a threatened center of endemism on southern Luzon Island, Philippines. *Fieldiana: Zoology* (in press).

Heaney, L.R., and P.D. Heideman. 1987. Philippine fruit bats, endangered and extinct. *Bats* 5: 3–5.

Heaney, L.R., P.D. Heideman, E.A. Rickart, R.B. Utzurrum, and J.S.H. Klompen. 1989. Elevational zonation of mammals in the central Philippines. *Journal of Tropical Ecology* 5: 259–280.

Heaney, L.R. and R.A. Mittermeier 1997. The Philippines, pp. 236–255. *In* R.A. Mittermeier, P. Robles Gil, and C.G. Mittermeier, eds., *Megadiversity: Earth's Biologically Wealthiest Nations*. CEMEX, Monterrey, Mexico. 501 pp.

Heaney, L.R., and E.A. Rickart. 1990. Correlations of clades and clines: Geographic, elevational, and phylogenetic distribution patterns among Philippine mammals, pp. 321–332. *In* G. Peters and R. Hutterer, eds., *Vertebrates in the Tropics*. Mus. Alexander Koenig, Bonn. 424 pp.

Heaney, L.R., and B.R. Tabaranza, Jr. 1997. A preliminary report on mammalian diversity and conservation status of Camiguin Island, Philippines. *Sylvatrop* (1995) 5: 57–64.

Heaney, L.R., and R.C.B. Utzurrum. 1992. A review of the conservation status of Philippine land mammals. *Association of Systematic Biologists of the Philippines Communications* (1991) 3: 1–13.

Heideman, P.D. 1988. The timing of reproduction in the fruit bat, *Haplonycteris fischeri* (Pteropodidae): Geographic variation and delayed development. *Journal of Zoology* (London) 215: 577–595.

Heideman, P.D. 1989. Delayed development in Fischer's pygmy fruit bat, *Haplonycteris fischeri*, in the Philippines. *Journal of Reproduction and Fertility* 85: 363–382.

Heideman, P.D., and K.R. Erickson. 1987. The climate and hydrology of the Lake Balinsasayao watershed, Negros Oriental, Philippines. *Silliman Journal* 34: 82–107.

Heideman, P.D., and L.R. Heaney. 1989. Population biology and estimates of abundance of fruit bats (Pteropodidae) in Philippine submontane rainforest. *Journal of Zoology* (London) 218: 565–586.

Holttum, R.E. 1963. Cyatheacaea. *Flora Malesiana* II, 1: 65–176.

Ingle, N.R. 1992. The natural history of bats on Mt. Makiling, Luzon Island, Philippines. *Silliman Journal* 36: 1–26.

Ingle, N.R. 1993. Vertical stratification of bats in a Philippine rainforest. *Asia Life Sciences* 2: 215–222.

Ingle, N.R., and L.R. Heaney. 1992. A key to the bats of the Philippine Islands. *Fieldiana: Zoology* (n.s.) 69: 1–44.

Karnow, S. 1989. *In Our Image: America's empire in the Philippines*. Random House, New York. 494 pp.

Kummer, D.M. 1992. *Deforestation in the Postwar Philippines*. University of Chicago Press. 177 pp.

Kummer, D.M., and B.L. Turner II. 1994. The human causes of deforestation in Southeast Asia. *Bioscience* 44: 323–328.

Lepiten, M.V. 1997. The mammals of Siquijor Island, central Philippines. *Sylvatrop* (1995) 1 & 2: 1–17.

Magsalay, P.M. 1993. Rediscovery of four Cebu endemic birds (Philippines). *Asia Life Sciences* 2: 141–148.

Manalo, E.B. 1956. The distribution of rainfall in the Philippines. *Philippine Geographical Journal* 4: 104–166.

Merrill, E.D. 1923–26. *An Enumeration of Philippine Flowering Plants*. Manila, Bureau of Printing.

Merrill, E.D. 1945. *Plant Life of the Pacific World*. MacMillan Co., New York. 295 pp.

Musser, G.G., and P.W. Freeman. 1981. A new species of *Rhynchomys* (Muridae) from the Philippines. *Journal of Mammalogy* 62: 154–159.

Musser, G.G., and L.R. Heaney. 1992. Philippine rodents: Definitions of *Tarsomys* and *Limnomys* plus a preliminary assessment of phylogenetic patterns among native Philippine murines (Murinae, Muridae). *Bulletin of the American Museum of Natural History* 211: 1–138.

Musser, G.G., L.R. Heaney, and B.R. Tabaranza, Jr. A new species of *Batomys* (Mammalia, Muridae) from Dinagat Island, Philippines. *American Museum Novitates* (in press).

Myers, N. 1984. *The Primary Source: Tropical forests and our future*. W.W. Norton & Co., New York. 399 pp.

Myers, N. 1988. Environmental degradation and some economic consequences in the Philippines. *Environmental Conservation* 15: 205–214.

Myers, N. 1993. *Ultimate Security: The environmental basis of political stability*. W.W. Norton & Co., New York. 308 pp.

National Mapping and Resource Information Authority. 1988. Sheet maps, 1:250,000, based on satellite images from the Swedish Space Corporation. Manila, 53 sheets.

Oliver, W.L.R., C.R. Cox, and C.P. Groves. 1993b. The Philippine warty pigs (*Sus philippensis* and *Sus cebifrons*). *In* Oliver, W.L.R., ed., *Pigs, Peccaries, and Hippos: Status survey and conservation action plan*. IUCN, Gland, 202 pp.

Oliver, W.L.R., M.L. Dolar, and E. Alcala. 1992. The Philippine spotted deer, *Cervus alfredi* Sclater, conservation program. *Silliman Journal* 36: 47–54.

Oliver, W.L.R., C.R. Cox, P.C. Gonzales, and L.R. Heaney. 1993. Cloud rats in the Philippines: Preliminary report on distribution and status. *Oryx* 27: 41–48.

Oliver, W.L.R., and L.R. Heaney. 1996. Biodiversity and conservation in the Philippines. *International Zoo News* 43: 329–337.

Peterson, A.T., and L.R. Heaney. 1993. Genetic differentiation in Philippine bats of the genera *Cynopterus* and *Haplonycteris*. *Biological Journal of the Linnean Society* 49: 203–218.

Porter, G., and D.J. Ganapin, Jr. 1988. *Resources, Population, and the Philippines Future: A case study*. World Resources Institute, Washington. 68 pp.

Rabor, D.S. 1955. Notes on mammals and birds of the central northern Luzon highlands, Philippines. Pt. 1. Notes on mammals. *Silliman Journal* 2: 193–218.

Rabor, D.S. 1966. A report on the zoological expeditions in the Philippines for the period 1961–1966. *Silliman Journal* 13: 604–616.

Rabor, D.S. 1977. *Philippine Birds and Mammals*. University of Philippines Press, Quezon City. 283 pp.

Regalado, J.C. 1995. Revision of the Philippine Medinilla. *Blumea* 40: 113–193.

Remigio, A.A. Jr. 1993. Philippine forest resource policy in the Marcos and Aquino governments: A comparative assessment. *Global Ecology and Biogeography Letters* 3: 192–193.

Repetto, R. 1988. *The forest for the trees? Government policies and the misuse of forest resources*. World Resources Institute, Washington. 105 pp.

Rickart, E.A. 1993. Diversity patterns of mammals along elevational and diversity gradients in the Philippines: Implications for conservation. *Asia Life Sciences* 2: 251–260.

Rickart, E.A., L.R. Heaney, D.S. Balete, and B.R. Tabaranza, Jr. A review of the genera *Crunomys* and *Archboldomys* (Rodentia, Muridae, Murinae) with descriptions of two new species from the Philippines. *Fieldiana: Zoology* (in press).

Rickart, E. A., L. R. Heaney, P. D. Heideman, and R. C. B. Utzurrum. 1993. The distribution and ecology of mammals on Leyte, Biliran, and Maripipi islands, Philippines. *Fieldiana Zoology* (new series) 72: 1–62.

Rickart, E.A., L.R. Heaney, and R.B. Utzurrum. 1991. Distribution and ecology of small mammals along an elevational transect in southeastern Luzon, Philippines. *Journal of Mammalogy* 72: 458–469.

Samson, D.A., E.A. Rickart, and P.C. Gonzales. 1997. Ant diversity and abundance along an elevational gradient in the Philippines. *Biotropica* 29: 349–363.

Santos, J.V. 1986. Philippine bamboos. In *Guide to Philippine Flora and Fauna* IV: 1–43.

Tan, B.C., E.S. Fernando, and J.P. Rojo. 1986. An updated list of endangered Philippine plants. *Yushiana* 3(2): 1–5.

Tan, B.C., and Z. Iwatsuki. 1991. A new annotated Philippine moss checklist. *Harvard Papers in Botany* 3: 1–64.

Utzurrum, R.C.B. 1992. Conservation status of Philippine fruit bats (Pteropodidae). *Silliman Journal* 36: 27–45.

Utzurrum, R.C.B. 1995. Feeding ecology of Philippine fruit bats: Patterns of resource use and seed dispersal, pp. 63–77. *In* Racey, P.A., and S.M. Swift, eds., *Ecology, Evolution, and Behaviour of Bats*. Symposia of the Zoological Society of London 67: 1–421.

Vitug, M.D. 1993. *Power from the Forest: The politics of logging*. Philippine Center for Creative Journalism, Manila. 277 pp.

Whitmore, T.C. 1984. *Tropical Rain Forests of the Far East*. Clarendon Press, Oxford. 352 pp.

Wildlife Conservation Society of the Philippines. 1997. *Philippine Red Data Book*. Bookmark, Inc., Makati City. 262 pp.

World Bank. 1989. *Philippines: Environment and Natural Resource Management Study*. The World Bank, Washington. 170 pp.

INDEX